Discovering Your Couple
Sexual Style

D0112241

Discovering Your Couple
Sexual Style

Sharing Desire, Pleasure, and Satisfaction

Barry W. McCarthy
Emily McCarthy

Routledge
Taylor & Francis Group
New York   London

Routledge
Taylor & Francis Group
270 Madison Avenue
New York, NY 10016

Routledge
Taylor & Francis Group
2 Park Square
Milton Park, Abingdon
Oxon OX14 4RN

© 2009 by Taylor & Francis Group, LLC
Routledge is an imprint of Taylor & Francis Group, an Informa business

Printed in the United States of America on acid-free paper
10 9 8 7 6 5 4 3 2

International Standard Book Number-13: 978-0-415-99469-9 (Softcover)

Library of Congress Cataloging-in-Publication Data

McCarthy, Barry W., 1943-
    Discovering your couple sexual style : sharing desire, pleasure, and satisfaction /
Barry McCarthy and Emily McCarthy.
        p. cm.
    ISBN 978-0-415-99469-9 (pbk. : alk. paper)
    1. Couples--Sexual behavior. 2. Sex instruction. 3. Sexual excitement. 4. Intimacy
(Psychology) 5. Sex in marriage. 6. Man-woman relationships. I. McCarthy, Emily J. II.
Title.

HQ31b.M137 2009
613.9'6--dc22   2008030589

Visit the Taylor & Francis Web site at
http://www.taylorandfrancis.com

and the Routledge Web site at
http://www.routledge.com

Contents

Part III Surmounting Sexual Challenges

Part IV Maintaining Healthy Couple Sexuality

Introduction

We are glad that you have turned to *Discovering Your Couple Sexual Style* as a guide to help you choose what is right for you and your intimate relationship. This book has been a joy for us to write, and we hope it will be an engaging and worthwhile book for you to read and utilize in your lives.

The theme of this book is helping you discover and enjoy your couple sexual style so that it plays a vibrant role in energizing your bond and contributing to couple satisfaction. In it, we discuss differences in sexual desire; differentiate between the role and meaning of spontaneous vs. planned lovemaking; explore psychological, medical, and relational factors in sexuality; and help you develop positive, realistic expectations for sexuality in your relationship. We ask that you ignore what you see about sex on TV, disregard romantic movies, and close your Internet porn site. Truth, you will come to realize, is much more satisfying than fiction.

The authors have been married for more than 40 years and view sexuality as a vital, integral part of our marital bond. We wish we'd had a book like this when we started as a couple since our early sexual experiences were typified by high-frequency, low-quality sex. It took us more than two years to develop a couple sexual style that was mutually satisfying. We continue to refine our couple sexual style to this day.

This is our eleventh co-authored book. We have spent more than three years researching and writing *Discovering Your Couple Sexual Style*. It is our favorite book because it emphasizes primary prevention by urging you to develop a strong, resilient couple sexual style rather than relying on unrealistic concepts of sexuality. This book can also help couples who suffer from sexual dissatisfaction and dysfunction address these problems by developing a couple sexual style that integrates intimacy and eroticism.

This allows sexuality to play a positive role in promoting relationship vitality and satisfaction.

A theme of our books, whether the topic is relationships or sex, is taking personal responsibility and working as an intimate team to make "wise" sexual and relationship decisions. Positive motivation and understanding promotes wise choices while guilt, shame, or anxiety about yourself or the past subverts self-esteem, your relationship, and sexuality.

A significant part of Barry's clinical practice involves couples suffering from inhibited desire and other sexual problems. He has treated more than 4,000 individuals and couples with sexual concerns and dysfunction. Typically, the sexual problems have gone on for years, and the couple feels demoralized and stigmatized. They mistakenly believe that they are the only couple with this problem and approach therapy with a great deal of embarrassment and hesitancy.

Our motivation for writing this book was to provide knowledge, support, and hope for married couples and those in serious relationships. You can successfully address intimacy and sexual issues whether the problems are acute and minor or severe and chronic. Each couple can develop their own unique sexual style that promotes desire, pleasure, and satisfaction. Sexuality can and should play a 15–20% positive role in your intimate relationship.

Audience for and Structure of the Book

Discovering Your Couple Sexual Style is for you if you are:

- About to be married, newly married, or in a serious, intimate relationship.
- In a committed relationship free of sexual difficulties or problems and are searching for ways to improve or maintain the quality of your couple sexuality.
- Either married or in a serious relationship and have a sex life that is dissatisfying or dysfunctional. You're looking for a way to make your sexual relationship vital and satisfying.
- Over 50, find your old ways of approaching sex are no longer working, and feel the need to develop a new couple sexual style.

We have strived to provide information, guidelines, exercises, and case studies to help you, individually and as committed partners, find your own sexual voice and develop a satisfying couple sexual style. If your goal is to accept and enjoy your sexuality, you've come to the right book. And we respect you greatly for being here.

This is a self-help book, not a substitute for individual, marital, or sex therapy. We offer information, guidelines, case examples, exercises, personal observations, and suggest change strategies and techniques. Increasing awareness and reducing myths and stigmas are crucial to strengthen relationships, but sometimes this is not enough. Appendix A provides information and resources for addressing intimacy and sexual problems with professional help, which is often the wisest approach.

Do not read this book as if it were a textbook that requires you to go through it chapter by chapter. Each chapter is self-contained. We suggest reading chapters that are most relevant to your situation, and decide whether the guidelines are personally relevant for you. Most chapters include a case study. These are composite cases of couples Barry has seen in his practice, with names and details altered to protect confidentiality. Case studies demonstrate that real-life couples have problems that can be resolved. We urge you to make reading this book an active, involving learning experience by discussing it with your partner, trying relevant assessment and change exercises, and integrating new sexual attitudes, experiences, and feelings into your couple sexual style.

We hope this book will provide a challenging, supportive structure and motivate you to develop a unique couple sexual style that will enhance intimacy, pleasure, eroticism, and sexual satisfaction.

PART I
Developing a Healthy Couple Sexuality

CHAPTER 1

Establishing Positive, Realistic Sexual Expectations

Jeffrey and Marge were very animated as they left the movie theater after seeing *Pretty Woman*. The lovemaking scenes in this R-rated movie were hot and inviting. Jeffery said, "How come we don't have great sex? Why can't you be like Julia Roberts?" Marge's mood immediately changed. She felt attacked, so she counterattacked by saying, "Why can't you be successful, wealthy, and sexy like Richard Gere?" Within five minutes the good feelings had disappeared, and Jeffrey and Marge were back in the familiar attack–counterattack mode that occurred whenever they talked about their sexual relationship. How can something that should be so natural and loving turn into a source of negativity and frustration? About half the couples reading about Jeffrey and Marge think, "I'm glad we don't have those kinds of sexual problems." Unfortunately, the other half of you identify, to a greater or lesser extent, with their sexual disappointment and frustration.

Not All Sex Is Great Sex

Think all sex should be earth shattering? The quality of most couple sex doesn't measure up to Hollywood images, so people feel deficient or even dysfunctional. We are avid moviegoers, but realize that sex in movies isn't based on reality. In movies, both people are totally desirous and turned on before any touching occurs; the sex is intense, short, non-verbal; and everyone has multiple orgasms. This is a powerful but very distorted image of the perfect romantic love/passionate sex encounter. And, by the way, movie sex usually does not involve married couples but a new couple or an extra-marital affair. It's a totally erroneous message for real-life couples like yourselves.

Here's a survey to assess your beliefs regarding sex and sexuality. This True–False test identifies your attitudes, knowledge, and feelings about couple sex.

1. Each sexual experience should involve mutual desire and arousal.
2. It is crucial for the woman to be orgasmic at each sexual encounter.
3. Sexually satisfied couples have simultaneous orgasms at least half the time.
4. The more intimate the couple, the more erotic the sex is.
5. In order to have a satisfying sexual encounter, both people should feel desirous before touching begins.
6. The male has to be receptive every time the female initiates sex.
7. Each touching experience should proceed to orgasm; if not, one (or both) partners will feel cheated.
8. Fantasizing about another person means you want to have an affair.
9. Afterplay is only necessary if the woman has not been orgasmic.
10. Feelings of disappointment or anger must be resolved before being sexual.
11. If 10% of sexual encounters are dissatisfying or dysfunctional, this signals a major sexual problem.
12. If one person wants to use erotic videos or sex toys, this is a sign of lack of attraction.
13. As long as you love each other and keep lines of communication open, sex will be fine.
14. It's better if the man is the sexual initiator.
15. If you aren't having sex at least three times a week, you have inhibited sexual desire.

The test you just finished is a sex myth test. Based on the best research and clinical experience available, the correct answer to each question is "False." Believing in these and other myths interferes with your ability to develop a satisfying couple sexual style. We confront these myths in the chapters that follow, but consider, for starters, some real-life facts about couple sex:

- Less than 50% of the time will happily married, sexually satisfied couples describe a particular sexual experience as equally and mutually satisfying.
- In 25% of sexual encounters, one partner finds the sex positive while the other feels it was okay. Usually it is the man who is more satisfied. These experiences might not be "scene stealers," but they are good for your intimate relationship.

- Fifteen percent of sexual encounters are functional but unremarkable. If you had to do it over again, you probably would have decided to watch Jay Leno instead.
- The most important statistic to remember is that 5–15% of sexual experiences of normal, healthy, happy couples are dissatisfying or dysfunctional.

Keep this information in mind as you strive to keep up with the media image of great sex. You cannot compare your experiences with media myths or couples who brag they have multi-orgasmic sex each night. Most folks were fed either no or bad information about sex and are paying the price years later in relationship dissatisfaction caused, in part, by wildly unrealistic expectations.

Contrary to media myths, the truth is that there is not one right way to be sexual. If two people are content with having intercourse twice a month that can be as healthy as the couple who strives for mutual orgasms three times a week. There is no absolute sexual right or wrong. You have to determine what is comfortable and satisfying for you, individually and as a couple.

Exercise: Realistic Expectations

As you review the sex myth test, you and your partner can write the three to five myths that have had the most negative influence on your views of sexuality.

My most influential myths	My partner's most influential myths
_____	_____
_____	_____
_____	_____
_____	_____
_____	_____

Now discuss these. Are you hurt or angry about the power these myths have had over you, your sexuality, and your relationship? Confronting these myths is necessary, but not sufficient. Don't replace myths with "socially desirable" responses. What are the positive, realistic understandings and expectations that will enhance your life and facilitate healthy, satisfying sexuality in your relationship?

Think about an enticing movie (or magazine) moment that was highly charged for you, and that you believed was the sexual ideal. Some will remember the love scene from *Titanic*, others a scene from *Debbie Does Dallas*. Is there any reality to this "Hollywood moment?" How has this fantasy image of sexuality affected your sexual expectations and satisfaction? Discuss your thoughts and perceptions of this cinematic sexual encounter with your partner. Even more important, talk with your partner about a new couple approach to sexual expectations and satisfaction. If you want, get the DVD and look at it from both the fantasy and the realistic perspective. Remember, movies rarely feature married or serious couples. Realize that this is entertainment, not a healthy lesson in couple sexuality and satisfaction. As you read *Discovering Your Couple Sexual Style* be open to talking about concepts, guidelines, exercises, and case studies with your partner. Be prepared to replace Hollywood expectations with something more real and more satisfying: a solid understanding of how to develop your unique couple sexual style and maintain positive, realistic sexual expectations.

Three Guidelines for Sexual Satisfaction

No amount of expertise and research can tell you the right way to be sexual. But we can help you discover the sexual satisfaction that is unique to you and your relationship. Creating your couple sexual style depends on three core guidelines. The good news is that these guidelines are easy to follow. We utilize these guidelines throughout the book and relate them to your personal and couple sexuality. As you master and apply these concepts, you will be able to create a lifetime of quality couple sex in a genuinely intimate relationship.

Guideline 1: Develop positive, realistic sexual expectations   The Hollywood version of great sex is of the perfect romantic love/passionate sex encounter. This image—universal as it may be—sets a standard that no real life couple can, or should, strive to attain. To experience genuine sexual satisfaction, it is essential that you throw out the media-driven notion of what great sex ought to be. When it comes to satisfying sex, you can develop your own positive, realistic script (expectations).

Guideline 2: Sensual and sexual options   Sex is not synonymous with intercourse. Couples who create a vital, intimate connection learn that the penis and vagina are not the only body parts involved in sex. Healthy couple sexuality involves many options, and intercourse is only one of those options. Using both your body and your mind opens up a range of sensual and sexual pleasures to help develop a broad, variable, flexible sexual relationship that fits the realities of your life, feelings, and situation.

Guideline 3: Communicate sexual desires   You have preferences about what you want to share sexually with your partner. Your mate has preferences of his or her own. The pathway to sexual satisfaction is to be open to each other's feelings, needs, and preferences. There's a lot going on in your partner's mind and body, feelings and preferences you probably are not aware of. Hollywood notions of romantic love and passionate sex require that you instinctively "know" your lover's needs without words or guidance. In reality, getting to know your partner's sexual feelings and needs requires both verbal and emotional communication, which is best done outside the bedroom so you can focus on learning your mate's distinctive non-verbal cues.

Closing Thoughts

A vital couple sexuality motivates you to address relationship issues and build a respectful, trusting, and intimate bond. A core strategy in building and maintaining a strong, resilient bond is your ability to deal with differences and conflicts. Couples find that only about 30% of conflicts are truly resolvable, 50–60% are modifiable, and 10–20% need to be accepted without it controlling your view of your partner or relationship.

Learning to accept and maintain positive, realistic expectations of your partner, relationship, and sexuality is a core element in couple satisfaction. In this book we focus primarily on intimacy and sexuality, but many of these concepts and guidelines are also applicable to your general relationship. A healthy relationship is based on a positive-influence process, which brings out the best in each person and contributes to personal, relational, and sexual well-being and satisfaction. You want sexuality to play a healthy 15–20% role in energizing your bond and increasing feelings of desire and desirability.

CHAPTER **2**

Determining Your Couple Sexual Style

There are as many approaches to sex as there are couples. In truth, there is no one right way to be sexual. So what is a couple sexual style? Each couple develops a unique expression of sexuality, which is neither static nor totally predictable. The core issue is how you integrate intimacy and eroticism into your couple sexuality. Your sexual style is likely to evolve as your interests, preferences, and experiences change. You forge a sexual style based on your needs and preferences—both as individuals and as an intimate team. We will coach you in choosing a sexual style that is comfortable and functional for you. Developing your unique couple sexual style will enhance sexual desire, pleasure, and satisfaction.

The first element in your couple sexual style is intimacy. Humans differ from animals in their need for emotional connection and their desire to enhance and maintain emotional closeness. Intimacy is the emotional component of healthy couple sexuality. It allows you to feel safe in your sexual relationship. Intimacy usually involves affectionate, and often sensual, touch. Empathy for your partner's feelings and sharing a range of emotions and experiences are core qualities of intimacy. Of course, you won't forget the first time you made love; however, just as important are the fond recollections of walks on the beach, meaningful conversations that extended into the night, lying together watching a video while talking and touching. Those are the special feelings and experiences of intimacy.

The second component of your couple sexual style is eroticism. Both women and men desire sexual connection, arousal, and orgasm. From the first time you heard or fantasized about feeling desired and desirable, you felt an erotic charge. Erotic feelings may or may not have been attached to an

9

emotional relationship. It is normal to feel a desire for sexual expression—from reading sexy novels to having erotic fantasies during masturbation and sexual urges when "making out" in a car. Sexual pleasure and eroticism is a healthy component of your sexual self, especially in an intimate relationship.

The challenge of developing your couple sexual style is to integrate intimacy and eroticism. Some women, for example, enjoy intimacy and touching with their spouse but feel inhibited with erotic expression, wrongly believing that is the man's domain. Many men feel intimacy is the woman's domain and try to show intimacy to please her. The reality is that both men and women can learn to value both intimacy and eroticism. The challenge for couples, married and unmarried, is to integrate these dimensions into their relationship.

What Is Your Couple Sexual Style?

Each couple develops its own sexual style. A core dimension is how emotionally close you want to feel and how much you value retaining your autonomy. The challenge of a healthy couple sexual style is for each partner to maintain individuality and at the same time experience being part of an intimate, erotic sexual team. You can develop a mutually comfortable level of intimacy that promotes sexual desire, facilitates eroticism, and energizes your relationship.

The following survey will help you focus on finding the right sexual style for you. Answer each question independently, even if it's a "we" question. Be honest and blunt; don't give "socially desirable" answers. This is about your personal preferences; you will discuss similarities and differences with your partner later. Answer the questions using a scale from 1 – 3: 1 = Disagree/Not like me; 2 = Sometimes agree; 3 = Agree/Very much like me.

1. I have to feel emotionally close to my partner before being sexual.
2. Sex isn't satisfying unless we take turns arousing each other.
3. I like strong emotions (both positive and negative); it makes me feel more sexually alive.
4. I value clear gender roles, especially the man's role to initiate sex.
5. I always think of my partner as my best friend.
6. I don't enjoy sex unless both of us have the same sexual needs, and can voice them in a positive manner.
7. I like to do erotic role-play, such as master–slave or virgin–prostitute.
8. Sex toys, or other external stimuli, have no place in our relationship.

9. I don't mind that sex doesn't happen frequently; the quality of our emotional relationship is much more important than the quantity of sex.
10. It's okay to have sex as a tension reducer.
11. Sexuality is all about feeling emotionally attached; if that doesn't happen it's not good sex.
12. Men and women have very different sexual needs and feelings.
13. Sex loses value if we both don't come.
14. I need both verbal and non-verbal communication to feel sexually receptive and responsive.
15. Watching porn helps me get into a lustful mood.
16. I avoid letting go erotically because I'm afraid it will push my partner away.
17. The biggest turn-on is knowing my partner really is enjoying the sex.
18. Either one of us can initiate sex. If my partner isn't interested, he or she will say no and we will find another way to connect.
19. Sex is a great way to make up after an argument.
20. Initiating affection is her domain, his is initiating intercourse.
21. If I don't feel emotionally bonded at the moment, having sex is meaningless.
22. We have distinct "his," "hers," and "our" ways to initiate a sexual encounter.
23. I enjoy feeling randy and lustful.
24. Once we begin to cuddle, I know that sex is either desired or expected.
25. We often consider having sex, but decide we'd rather talk and hang out.
26. I can offer a sexual option if I don't want to have intercourse.
27. One of the best things about sex is spontaneity and unpredictability.
28. I find pornography objectionable; it is not part of our sex life.
29. Sex is not about erotic cravings; its real purpose is an expression of emotional closeness.
30. We enjoy playing different roles when we act out erotic scenarios.
31. Sex is best after a bottle of wine; then I can really let go.
32. I like intercourse sex best, especially the man-on-top position.
33. The only meaningful sex is when we both feel emotionally connected and erotic at the same time; otherwise it's not worthwhile.
34. Sometimes I like to "talk dirty," and other times my partner likes to watch erotic videos.
35. We use make-up sex after a fight; this is a turn-on and heals the rift between us.
36. Foreplay is primarily for her, intercourse for him.

Defining Your Sexual Style: Scoring Key

	Yours	Partner's
Question 2	_____	_____
Question 6	_____	_____
Question 10	_____	_____
Question 14	_____	_____
Question 18	_____	_____
Question 22	_____	_____
Question 26	_____	_____
Question 30	_____	_____
Question 34	_____	_____
Total	C Style	
Question 4	_____	_____
Question 8	_____	_____
Question 12	_____	_____
Question 16	_____	_____
Question 20	_____	_____
Question 24	_____	_____
Question 28	_____	_____
Question 32	_____	_____
Question 36	_____	_____
Total	T Style	

	Yours	**Partner's**
Question 1	_____	_____
Question 5	_____	_____
Question 9	_____	_____
Question 13	_____	_____
Question 17	_____	_____
Question 21	_____	_____
Question 25	_____	_____
Question 29	_____	_____
Question 33	_____	_____
Total	F Style	
Question 3	_____	_____
Question 7	_____	_____
Question 11	_____	_____
Question 15	_____	_____
Question 19	_____	_____
Question 23	_____	_____
Question 27	_____	_____
Question 31	_____	_____
Question 35	_____	_____
Total	E Style	

Now place the totals for each style on the grid below.

	C Style	T Style	S Style	E Style
My Score				
Partner's Score				
Combined Score				

What was your highest score: C, T, S, or E?

What was your partner's highest score?

When you combine your scores, what style reflects your combined preferences?

The purpose of this survey is to help you answer the question of which couple sexual style best fits you. Your mate might have answered differently. It is normal for different people to have different feelings and preferences. Being a couple does not mean being clones of each other. Your combined score helps you assess how your couple style comes close to or differs from your preferred individual styles.

Understanding Your Sexual Compass

By completing this survey you have identified specific individual and couple preferences that influence your sexual style. Consider the issue of style as you would points on a compass. Let's examine each point and explore what this means in choosing a mutually comfortable and functional couple sexual style that's right for you.

C—Complementary Style: Mine and ours

T—Traditional Style: Conflict-Minimizing

F—Soulmate Style: Close and intimate

E—Emotionally Expressive Style: Fun and erotic

There is no "right" style that fits all couples. The key is to choose a mutually comfortable level of intimacy that allows each person to feel and express sexual desire. Each style has its strengths as well as vulnerabilities (traps).

Let's examine each point on the style compass. Remember, most couples do not have a "pure" style; rather, they develop a predominant approach that meets their needs for intimacy and eroticism. As your relationship changes, you can make adjustments and modifications in your couple sexuality. Most couples, however, maintain their core style because it is comfortable and allows them to share desire, pleasure, and satisfaction.

Complementary Style (C)   The complementary style allows each partner to have a positive sexual voice, as well as share as an intimate team. It is the most common sexual style. Couples who choose the complementary style realize that the best aphrodisiac is an involved, aroused partner. You don't expect your mate to create sexual magic; each person is responsible for his or her desire, arousal, and orgasm from the first cues of sexual desire to the last moments of orgasm.

Couples who choose the "mine and ours" style find that it provides a healthy integration of personal responsibility and being part of an intimate team. It is not your partner's role to give you desire or orgasm, but, as your intimate friend, your partner is receptive and responsive to your sexual feelings and preferences. Each partner feels free to initiate intimacy or to say no and is comfortable requesting a different sensual or erotic scenario. The couple can enjoy pleasure/eroticism, take turns choosing when to transition to intercourse, and enjoy a favorite afterplay scenario.

Strengths: With the one–two approach of personal responsibility and acting as an intimate team, this style's major strength is the variability and flexibility of sexual roles. Each person values intimacy and eroticism, each person has bridges to sexual desire, and sexuality is a shared experience leading to high levels of satisfaction.

Vulnerabilities: There are potential pitfalls with this style, as with other styles. Sex can fall into a routine, remaining functional, but with lower quality than desired. Lack of engagement and growth can lead to diminished desire and eroticism. When couples take sex and each other for granted, they become disappointed with the quality of their intimate relationship, and frustration and alienation ensues.

Traditional Style (T)   The traditional sexual style is the most predictable and stable. It puts a high premium on keeping the peace, valuing commitment and stability. The theme is "acceptance and security." Couples who adopt this style worry about emotional and sexual conflict; they are not into drama. They prefer continuity and traditional gender roles.

In the conflict-minimizing relationship, sex is usually the man's domain rather than shared. Affection and emotional intimacy is the woman's domain. Strong emotional expression is discouraged, including erotic expression. This is the least intimate and erotic style, with sex given a lower priority.

Strengths: The biggest strengths are predictability and security. The man and woman have clearly defined roles. He is the sexual initiator; she is less active in erotic scenarios but is open to his preferences. Her role is to initiate affection and emotional intimacy. A strong advantage is that since the sexual rules and roles are clear, sex rarely becomes a volatile issue.

Vulnerabilities: This style doesn't work for many couples; there is not enough mutuality and sexual intimacy. Another concern is that as the couple ages, the traditional male approach to intercourse becomes more vulnerable. If they have to deal with unexpected difficulties such as an infertility problem or an extra-marital affair, these couples do not have the motivation or resources to address it. A particular concern for women is when the gender roles are so rigid that their need for affectionate and intimate connection is not validated.

More than those in any other couple style, the traditional couple resists change. Yet, the reality is that change happens, especially with aging. Both the man and woman need to maintain a genuine intimate sexual connection and be open to sexual changes.

Soulmate Style (S) For years, relationship experts advocated for the "perfect" couple sexual style—being soulmates. The highest possible level of intimacy and closeness was the ideal for loving sexuality.

The role of intimacy is to promote closeness and safety. Couples who adapt the soulmate style enjoy shared experiences and talk about their relationship. They share feelings, spend time together, and give high priority to meeting each others' needs. The belief that the soulmate style was the "right" one for all couples was based on a false assumption: the more the intimacy, the better the sex. Research has found this is a myth. Intimacy is only a part of the equation. The danger is that too much closeness and predictability can subvert sexuality. Soulmate partners can "de-eroticize" each other. The challenge is to find a mutually comfortable level of intimacy that facilitates both desire and eroticism.

Strengths: The advantages of this style are a sense of personal acceptance, feeling loved and accepted for who you really are, feeling desired and desirable, and not fearing judgment or rejection. When this couple style works well, it truly meets needs for intimacy and security.

Vulnerabilities: So why isn't the soulmate style right for most couples? Because you can be so close that you lose erotic feelings for your partner. Moreover, you worry so much about hurting your partner's feelings that you don't talk about sexual concerns until they've become a chronic, severe problem. Women especially feel disappointed and alienated that the promise of the soulmate relationship was not met.

As soulmates, you enjoy sharing positive experiences; however, you are reluctant to face the hard issues of life and your relationship. For example, even in closely connected couples, affairs occur. Of all the couple styles, the soulmate couple has the hardest time recovering from an affair. The injured partner feels so hurt and betrayed the he or she remains stuck in resentment.

Couples who choose the soulmate style need to be sure that there is enough autonomy to maintain their sexual voice and that both partners are committed to integrating intimacy and eroticism.

Emotionally Expressive Style (E)   This is the stuff of strong emotion and drama. Partners are free to share their passions, positive and negative, in word and deed. The emotionally expressive style is the most erotic style. Its sense of vitality and adventure includes using role enactment arousal. It is the most engaging, exciting, fun, and unpredictable couple sexual style.

Strengths: The strength of this style is openness to emotional and sexual expression. Partners experience high levels of spontaneity, fun, genuine emotional expression, and a vital eroticism. Yes, the partners fight, but they have the most resilient and engaging couple style. In fact, they frequently use sex to reconnect after a conflict.

Vulnerabilities: The biggest danger is that this style is highest in relational instability. Although couples with this style can experience high levels of eroticism and sexual frequency, the level of emotional intimacy and security is overwhelmed by the intensity of negative emotions. These partners "wear each other out" by the frequency of their emotional upheavals. Advocates of this fun, erotic style run a major risk of breaking personal boundaries, resulting in a high divorce rate. While they love the good times and the good sex, they can be critical and hurtful, especially around desire and performance issues. Emotionally expressive couples are prone to affairs, and although they are resilient and can recover, by the fifth affair the trust bond is shattered. To be successful, partners must honor personal boundaries and not "hit below the belt," especially when the issue involves sexuality.

Choosing Your Couple Sexual Style

The challenge of a successful couple sexual style is to find the right balance between maintaining individuality (your personal sexual voice) and feeling genuinely connected as an intimate team. Accepting and understanding your partner's feelings and preferences allows you to have a sense of what is right for your relationship, both emotionally and sexually. It is crucial that you be true to the core components of your sexual voice so that you can develop a genuine couple style.

You can begin to develop your unique couple sexual style by exploring and sharing your sexual desires, feelings, and preferences. Remember, being intimate, erotic sexual friends is very different than being clones of each other. Your preferences and sensitivities are part of who you are as a sexual person and can be integrated into your couple sexual style so that you can share intimacy, desire, pleasure, eroticism, and satisfaction.

You may be concerned that you don't have the exact same preferences as your partner or even that you have very different settings on the compass. Don't panic. Differences are important and need to be explored. It is common for individuals to struggle with differences in intimacy and eroticism needs. If you are not able to understand and gain acceptance of the differences, you are strongly advised to seek professional help. Appendix A provides guidance in choosing a couple sex therapist.

Linda and Ian Romantic love, passionate sex, and idealization are wonderful ways to start a relationship, and Linda and Ian love to recall their first six months as a couple. Linda felt she had found her "soulmate," and Ian was sure now that they were a couple he could have all the sex he wanted and there would be no conflicts of any kind. Unfortunately, romantic idealism is the enemy of developing a mutually satisfying couple sexual style.

When Linda and Ian came to Barry's office 19 months after marriage, they were a demoralized, alienated couple who had very little sex. Linda felt disappointed in Ian and the marriage, believing he was a sexually selfish man. Ian felt Linda had pulled a "bait and switch" about sex and that she promoted conflicts and problems as an excuse to avoid sex. In fact, Linda and Ian were good people who wanted a satisfying, stable marriage and a healthy sexual relationship; however, they had unrealistic expectations that led to self-defeating marital and sexual power struggles.

Barry focused them on the crucial task of developing a strong, resilient marital bond of respect, trust, and intimacy and finding a couple sexual style that was both intimate and erotic. This included giving up unrealistic and unhealthy demands on the spouse and marital sexuality.

Linda wanted a genuine emotional connection with Ian but had to accept that Ian was not her clone. Ian had his own way of expressing emotional and sexual intimacy. Ian had to realize that Linda was not a "sexual machine" and that affectionate, sensual, playful, and erotic touch had value other than just as "foreplay." Ian needed to realize that it is normal to have differences and conflicts emotionally, practically, and sexually. Sharing your lives and bodies is a complex, multi-dimensional process. Conflict resolution and problem solving both inside and outside the bedroom is a core component of a healthy marriage and healthy marital sexuality.

In therapy sessions, as well as talking at home and taking the inventory in this chapter, Linda and Ian chose the complementary couple sexual style as being best for them. Linda had her own "sexual voice," which meant her initiations of intimacy were quite different than Ian's. She valued broad-based touch, and Ian agreed that not all touch needed to proceed to intercourse and orgasm. Linda embraced her freedom to choose whether to become really involved in a sexual encounter, to "go along for the ride," to say no to sex and cuddle instead, or to enjoy pleasuring Ian to orgasm.

Linda felt she had influenced Ian to value affectionate, and erotic, non-intercourse touch. He'd always valued intercourse and she hoped in the future that Ian could learn to take pleasure in both giving and receiving sensual touch. Ian accepted that Linda was a pro-sexual woman whose sexuality was different and more complex than his. He was a smart man who realized that her variable, flexible approach to sexuality would serve them well in their later years. Ian was glad that their marriage was back on track and that sexuality now played a positive role in energizing their marital bond. He felt desirable, valued their complementary couple sexual style, and felt good about experiencing both intimacy and eroticism in marital sex.

Closing Thoughts

Each couple develops their own sexual style, which allows the partners to share intimacy and eroticism. To be truly satisfied sexually, you need to have a comfortable, pleasurable, and functional sexual style, which plays a 15–20% role in your relationship and promotes intimacy and security. Chapter 4 describes in greater detail the four couple styles and how to play to the strengths of each while avoiding the pitfalls. Take personal responsibility for your sexuality and share pleasure and eroticism as an intimate team. In sharing yourself emotionally and sexually, you will continue to enjoy healthy, satisfying couple sex.

CHAPTER 3

Communicating Your Sexuality

The Five Dimensions of Touch

When most people talk about sex they mean intercourse, which is, of course, an integral component of sex. However, there are many ways to be sexual, intercourse being only one of many. The essence of sex is giving and receiving pleasure-oriented touching, which includes affectionate, sensual, playful, erotic, and intercourse touch. When it is "intercourse or nothing," nothing eventually wins.

Healthy sexual couples learn to value a range of emotional and physical ways to connect and reconnect in order to maintain a vital, satisfying sexuality. The concept of non-demand pleasuring is particularly valuable for older couples. However, learning this technique in your twenties or thirties will inoculate you against sexual problems as you age. Non-demand pleasuring affirms the value of each non-intercourse touch dimension—affectionate, sensual, playful, and erotic—which helps maintain connection and promotes sharing yourself and your body. Touch counts, whether it eventually proceeds to intercourse or not. Touch is an invitation to share pleasure, not a demand for intercourse.

The concept of sensual and sexual options helps break the traditional male–female power struggle about sex. Typically, the man emphasizes intercourse and views touch as "foreplay," which makes the woman feel pressured rather than invited and ambivalent about initiating touch unless she wants to "go all the way." So both pleasurable touch and intercourse frequency are lost. With non-demand pleasuring and acceptance of sensual and sexual options, you have a "win–win" situation that helps facilitate both pleasure-oriented touching and intercourse. Contrary to media sexual performance myths (e.g., books and articles about how to have sex 365 days a year or ensure multi-orgasmic response every time), the average frequency of intercourse is once or twice a week, with the normal range being from once every two weeks to three times a week. So with intercourse or nothing, there is relatively little sensual or sexual touch. In truth, couple satisfaction would be higher with daily pleasurable touch and intercourse two or three times a week.

Enhancing sexual satisfaction is a process requiring time, energy, and focus. Depending on what you are doing and feeling, your level of sexual interest and energy will vary. This is normal, not a sign of a sexual problem. Even if you are in bed with your lover, with his or her body pressed tightly against you, you may or may not feel sexual desire. As you consider the potential discrepancy between your mate's interest and your own, it is of crucial importance to remember that you have options. Sex is not a power struggle of "intercourse or nothing."

One of the most common reasons for sexual power struggles is the idea that "sex" means an Academy Award–winning intercourse performance. In fact, sex often does not involve intercourse at all, and sometimes it involves merely "good enough" intercourse—better for one partner than the other.

Tina and Art

Tina understands the complexity and meaning of intimacy and sexuality. She's been with her husband, Art, for five years. "Between work and raising two young children often the most erotic intentions die out by the time we have space to do something more than a quick sexual touch when the kids aren't looking. We sometimes have gone three weeks without having any sex because by the time we are alone one or both of us are just too tired." It would be perfectly understandable if Tina gave up on sex because of the demands of her life. However, Tina did not fall into this trap of intercourse or nothing. She has learned to enjoy the give and take of a vital sexual life, recognizing that she and Art can feel good about their intimate connection, even given the reality of their daily life. They enjoy touching both inside and outside the bedroom. There are weeks when they will have sex three times, and weeks when they will not have intercourse but will keep a sensual and erotic connection.

Tina describes her strategy, which she and Art fashioned from an open attitude toward accommodating each other's feelings, preferences, and needs: "We have learned to accept the ebb and flow of sexual feelings as natural, real-life sex needs to fit into our real life. A 'no' is not taken as a personal rejection. I feel comfortable taking care of my sexual needs through masturbation on nights where I can see that Art is just too tired or distracted, and I am sure that Art has done the same. We go out of our way to do little things during the day to make each other feel desired and sexy, from embraces and loving words while making dinner to surprise oral sex while he's on the phone. We enjoy a range of sensual, playful, and erotic touch whenever we get the chance. Often, we know this will not lead to intercourse, but these little things build up and make us even more excited when we finally have the opportunity for intercourse."

Tina and Art have discovered one of the best ways to extricate their relationship from the ever-destructive sexual power struggle. They accept a key concept that escapes the attention of so many couples: Sex is much more than sexual intercourse. That's not to say that a touching experience doesn't often lead to intercourse, which is great. When both partners recognize that they can feel genuinely connected through a variety of intimate touching experiences, each will feel emotionally and sexually satisfied. Let's explore how the five dimensions of touch can help your relationship remain resilient and satisfying.

Getting Into Gear

We use the metaphor "gears of connection" to conceptualize the five dimensions of touch: (1) affection, (2) sensuality, (3) playfulness, (4) erotic non-intercourse, and (5) intercourse. Think of these dimensions of touch as the five gears of a stick shift car. You start in first gear and shift all the way to fifth gear. But there are situations in which you would not use fifth gear, e.g., if you were merely driving a couple of blocks under snowy conditions. Just as with finding the right gear of a car, you can find the right gear(s) of touch. To make these dimensions clearer and more concrete, think of arousal as a 10-point scale on which 0 is neutral, 5 marks the beginning of sexual arousal, and 10 is orgasm.

First Gear: Affectionate Touch Affectionate touch, gear one, involves enjoying the same warm, romantic experiences as when you first met and fell in love. These involve hands-on, clothes-on interactions—holding hands, kissing, and hugging. Affectionate touch is about feeling emotionally safe and connected, which facilitates each person's receptivity to sensual and sexual connection. This concept of affection is different than the mechanical hug or ritual goodbye kiss. Affectionate touch is a genuine reaching out. It is fascinating to realize that for some people the real emotional meaning of touch is conveyed by hand holding, while for others it is hugging or kissing that has a special symbolic meaning.

First gear is also far different than starting foreplay, which often rushes through kisses and hugs, moving quickly to intercourse. In terms of the arousal process, affectionate touch establishes a solid foundation of 1 on the 10-point scale. Affectionate touch provides an opportunity to take your time and really enjoy being with your partner. Knowing that you might not move out of this gear allows you to slow down and enjoy the ride.

What is your preferred way of expressing affection?

- Hand holding
- Hugging
- Kissing
- Walking arm in arm
- Letting legs or feet touch while sitting on the couch or at dinner

Do you prefer touching or being touched? Taking turns or mutual touch? How important is affectionate touch to you and your relationship? Affectionate touch is not sexual, but is an important dimension in your intimate relationship.

Second Gear: The Sensual Gear   Second gear involves sensual touch that can be done with clothes on, semi-clothed, or nude. Sensual touch can include whole body massage (except for genitals), stroking and holding your partner as you lie together on a rug in front of the fireplace, and other forms of sharing pleasure through non-genital touch. Sensuality is the foundation of sexual response. It promotes feelings in the 2–4 range of the 10-point scale, facilitating receptivity and response to pleasure-oriented touch. This experience is also called non-genital pleasuring. This is the time to connect in a way that can involve music and candles. In second gear you explore each other's bodies and enjoy giving and receiving nurturing touch. With sensual massage, you engage in slow, rhythmic touch of your partner's whole body, from the top of the head to the soles of the feet, except for genitals, breasts, and anal area. The focus is on warmth, closeness, nurturing, and pleasure rather than arousal. For example, Tina especially enjoys cuddling with Art when they awake and before getting the baby.

Examples of sensual second gear include the following:

- Cuddling on the couch while watching a DVD
- Kissing and touching before going to sleep
- Resting your head on your partner's shoulder or lap
- Cradling each other, with arms intertwined, on awakening
- Giving/getting a back rub

In the sex therapy world, we call this gear non-demand pleasuring. This means enjoying giving touch and pleasure and expecting nothing in return other than the good feelings of the touch. Neither of you demands that touch proceeds past second gear. The "give-to-get" guideline reinforces that the best way to receive pleasure is to give pleasure.

Third Gear: The Playful Gear   Third gear involves playful touch, which intermixes non-genital and genital touch. Partners can be nude or semi-clothed. While playful touch does not involve "sex" in the same way intercourse does, it can be fun and inviting, partly because of its unpredictability. Playful touch can include full body massage, showering or bathing together and playing with each other's bodies, engaging in seductive or erotic dancing, playing strip poker or even a silly game like "Twister." In terms of arousal, playful touch, a lighthearted invitation to share sexual pleasure, evokes feelings of 4–6 on the 10-point scale. In the sex therapy world, this is called genital pleasuring.

Tina talks about her enjoyment of playful touch even if, and perhaps especially if, intercourse is not the end result of the encounter. "It's fun to tease each other here and there all through the day, like on a date." Don't lose the chance to enjoy this gear for what it is. Yes, it's playful, but it serves a meaningful role by giving you a chance to enjoy each other as sexual beings. This is the gear in which you can pull out the silly sex game you got at your bridal shower or read to each other from *Passionate Hearts*, Wendy Maltz's book of romantic/sexual poems and stories. Nowhere is it truer than with playful touch that it's not whether you win or lose but how you play the game. Like the other gears, playful touch has value in itself, as well as serving as a bridge to sexual desire and intercourse.

Fourth Gear: The Erotic Gear   Fourth gear involves erotic non-intercourse touch. In some ways, this is the most challenging option for adult couples to enjoy without feeling unduly pressured to proceed to intercourse. Erotic non-intercourse touch can include manual, oral, rubbing, or vibrator stimulation to high arousal and orgasm for one or both partners. In terms of the arousal continuum, this gear involves an "erotic flow" from 7–10 on the 10-point scale. Many couples associate erotic non-intercourse scenarios with pre-marital or extra-marital couples, rather than married or serious couples who regularly have intercourse. We believe that erotic scenarios and techniques can be a vital resource for your couple sexual style. Erotic scenarios often lead to intercourse, but have value in themselves as an erotically expressive alternative to intercourse. Intercourse is a choice, not a mandate.

Once your clothes are off and before—or without—transitioning to intercourse, a world of erotic scenarios and techniques is open to you in fourth gear. Don't lose the chance to make the most of this opportunity. Even if intercourse doesn't happen, it can still be a great sexual night. Sometimes erotic activities sound edgy, like Tina giving oral sex when Art was on the phone. If you are uncomfortable with up-front eroticism, your inhibitions will interfere with your chance to explore this gear as much as you and your mate might like. Whether erotic sex is to your taste or not, what we ask is that you be aware of this option and keep open lines of communication about sexuality, which leads to discovering each other's preferred erotic scenarios and techniques. Erotic, non-intercourse sex offers a very valuable alternative scenario when a sexual encounter does not flow to intercourse.

Fifth Gear: Intercourse   When people think about "sex," this is the gear they think of. Fifth gear does involve intercourse, but it approaches intercourse differently than the concept of "sex equals intercourse." Intercourse is viewed as merely one of the dimensions of sensuality/sexuality. Some couples rush through the earlier gears in a race to intercourse (we call that sexual "drag racing"). If your partner likes a fast ride, you both may be very happy with your intercourse-focused sexual relationship. But most women (and most men who slow down long enough to admit it) find sex more personally fulfilling when they learn to view intercourse as a special pleasuring/erotic dimension of the touching experience.

Most couples learn to transition to intercourse as soon as they physically can—i.e., when the man feels the woman is "ready"—and when there is high enough arousal that they physically can proceed—i.e., a level of 5 on the 10-point scale. Wise couples enjoy savoring the erotic experience and do not transition to intercourse until they are highly aroused (7 or 8 on the 10-point scale), with openness to the woman's initiation and guiding intromission. Intercourse then occurs as part of the erotic flow. For those who enjoy multiple stimulation during the pleasuring phase, multiple stimulation during intercourse can enhance sexual function and satisfaction.

Rather than viewing intercourse as a pass–fail test, you can learn to value intercourse as the natural extension of the intimacy/pleasuring/eroticism process. This approach to intercourse is especially valuable for couples after the age of 50, for women experiencing sexual pain, and for men concerned with erectile anxiety or ejaculatory inhibition.

In high school, they used to call these five dimensions of touch "bases." If the runner got to third base but did not score, it didn't count for anything. The concept that the only goal is to score intercourse and orgasm has no place in healthy couple sexuality. When you value intimacy, affection, sensuality, playful touch, eroticism, and think of intercourse as a natural transition at high levels of erotic flow, you remove the pressure that makes sex a pass–fail test. Consider a broader, more flexible, more human definition of sex as giving and receiving pleasure-oriented touching. You "pass" if you have intercourse, and "pass" if you don't. In any gear, you and your intimate relationship win.

Any good therapist takes the time to learn from his clients the secrets of their success. So I asked Tina how she was so wise at 29 years old. Like most folks, it's an intelligence based on experience. "For Art and me marriage did not automatically enrich our sexual relationship. In working through our trials and reinforcing our commitment, we have learned to trust each other more. We needed six months to build a comfortable couple sexual style. The key was twofold. First, we don't take it personally if the spouse is too tired to respond to our sexual initiation (and we have been on both ends of the scenario). Second, we don't wait for 'time for sex' to show that we are attracted to and turned on by each other. We enjoy giving and receiving affectionate, sensual, playful, and erotic touch."

Exercise: Understanding Your Touch Gears

Complete the following chart separately and then share with your partner. Be honest with yourself. What is the current percentage of affectionate, sensual, playful, erotic, and intercourse touch you actually experience? Even more important, what is the amount and percentage of touch you want to experience? Don't worry, this isn't a binding contract; it's a way of getting in touch with your feelings, needs, and preferences so you can understand and satisfy each other.

Touch Type	Current percentage of all touch	Percentage of touch you want
Affectionate Touch		
Sensual Touch		
Playful Touch		
Erotic Touch		
Intercourse Touch		

The next phase of the exercise involves each partner choosing one type of touch he or she would like to increase. In the ensuing week, one person takes responsibility to initiate an encounter focusing on that type of touch. The person initiating decides whether the couple will take turns or engage in mutual touching. Couples who have a very predictable sexual style may wish to push the limits of the types of touch to which they are receptive and responsive.

For example, if you desire to increase sensual touch, one partner could initiate a massage date. Take responsibility for your pleasure. You could turn on soft music, use a scented lotion, or light candles if that would increase the sensual milieu. You have the option of a mutual massage or taking turns on separate occasions as giver and receiver.

Another example is to plan a playful touching encounter. The initiator decides whether to wear sexy clothing or be in the nude; the partner can decide whether the touching occurs in the shower or while dancing in the living room. Your partner can add components like body paint, or put honey or chocolate on your body and nibble it off.

During the next six months, each person can return to this chart and choose a different gear to explore. Some couples take turns on alternate months, and others make initiations each and every month. It is interesting that few people enjoy all five gears. The hope is that you learn to value at least three gears, and ideally four dimensions of touch. You want to confront and change the "intercourse or nothing" pattern. Replace it with a broad variable, flexible approach to sex that values sensual, playful, and erotic touch.

Remember, do not judge your partner because his or her preferences are different than yours. Each person has his/her sexual voice, which should be integrated into your couple sexual style. Agree that neither of you will be coerced into doing anything that is against your moral or religious beliefs, but that otherwise you will keep an open mind about ways to learn each other's feelings and preferences.

After six months, assess your current touch behavior and your ideal touch preferences. Redo the chart with your partner over a beer or hot chocolate. Talk about what you've learned. Compare notes about what went well, what works on occasion, and what doesn't interest you. What have you learned about yourself, your likes and dislikes? What did you learn about your partner's preferences and turn-offs? What felt really special and built your sense of satisfaction?

You can develop realistic expectation for the dimensions of touching. In truth, few couples are comfortable with all five touch gears. Traditionally, couples have only two gears—affection and intercourse. Your couple sexual style will be enhanced if you can adopt at least three gears—affection, playful touch, and intercourse. In our view, sensual, playful, erotic, and intercourse touch are all sexual. Hopefully, you will learn to be comfortable with four gears. Affectionate touch is a crucial gear that connects and anchors your relationship, but it is not the only gear other than intercourse. An approach of "intercourse or nothing" leaves partners too vulnerable, and eventually the outcome will be nothing. You should be aware of and comfortable with the concept that the essence of a vital sexual relationship involves giving and receiving pleasure-oriented touch. For that to be a reality rather than just a slogan, you need to complement affectionate touch with at least one additional gear and, ideally, two—sensual, playful, or erotic touch.

Exercise for Exploring Touch Options

Each person and each couple can develop their own unique approach to sensual and sexual options. This exercise involves two phases. The first requires that each partner identify his/her preferred touch options, as well as what (if any) options he or she wants to veto. Second, the couple should play out at least two and preferably all of the acceptable options.

When you choose preferred options, we suggest that you assume affectionate touch and intercourse touch. The question is what your other sensual and sexual preferences are. We advocate that each person identify at least one and up to five preferred options. Examples include sensual massage, manual or oral stimulation to orgasm for one or both of you, dancing, showering or bathing together in a seductive or playful manner, doing a striptease for your partner, playing out a sex fantasy scenario with a prohibition on intercourse, cuddling on the couch or in bed for 30 minutes, playing sexually in the car (while parked, not driving), pleasuring your partner to orgasm, "making out" as you watch a favorite R-rated video. From this same list, each person can choose one to three options they don't like, with the assurance that the partner will honor this veto with no hassle. Once you have a list that includes from two to ten sensual/sexual options, we urge you to make this personal and concrete by playing out as many of these options as you can in the next three months. Enjoy!

Communicating Your Touch Option Preferences

Communicating how you feel about touch options is one of the most difficult, and also one of the most crucial, factors in your couple sexual style. You fear that this will be an awkward, clinical conversation that will take away warmth and intimacy from your relationship. If someone could create a pill that facilitated awareness and comfort but did not result in a detached, clinical approach, that pill would sell millions of prescriptions and truly facilitate the intimate, erotic life of couples. Focus on increasing sexual comfort and communication, but beware of crossing the line to sexual anxiety or awkwardness. Nothing is more anti-erotic than self-consciousness. Perhaps the best time to discuss sexual options is a day before a sexual encounter and the best place is during a walk or over a glass of wine or tea at the kitchen table or on the porch. The worst time and place is while lying in bed nude after a dissatisfying sexual experience. People feel too emotionally vulnerable and can say or do things that harm sexual self-esteem and mar an intimate relationship.

Communicating your feelings about sexual options involves (1) learning how to make the sexual encounter mutual and arousing so you transition to intercourse at high levels of arousal; (2) enjoying her pleasure and arousal whether or not she is orgasmic; (3) indulging sometimes in a "quickie" intercourse; (4) switching to erotic non-intercourse sex; (5) having a one-way "giving" erotic experience; (6) using self-stimulation by one or both of you to achieve orgasm in front of your partner; (7) enjoying a playful touching date as valuable in and of itself; (8) enjoying a mutual or one-way sensual encounter; (9) taking a "raincheck" and being affectionate instead of having intercourse; (10) accepting that this was one of the 5–15% of encounters that is dissatisfying or dysfunctional and being able to shrug it off.

All ten of these options are part of a variable, flexible couple sexual style. Obviously the first option is optimal, but this occurs in less than 50% of encounters even among the most loving, sexually functional couples. In valuing your couple sexual style, we urge you to be both positive and realistic. Most couples are not comfortable with all ten options, but you will feel better about your intimate, erotic relationship if you are comfortable with at least 3–4 options, and ideally 6–8. When the goal is sexual satisfaction in a serious relationship, having a range of options is superior to "intercourse or nothing."

Claudia and Felix   Claudia and Felix have been married 11 years and feel their sexual relationship is more mature and satisfying than ever. They met in college and were viewed by friends as a typical roller-coaster dating couple. Romantic love/passionate sex were intermixed with tearful break-ups accompanied by accusations and counter-accusations. A roommate said watching them was more entertaining than the TV show *Friends*. The drama and jealousy served as an erotic charge for their relationship, but it was a major emotional drain. They began to lose respect for each other and their relationship. Felix's father and Claudia's mother lobbied their respective children to "move on."

The issue was brought to a head when Claudia was admitted to medical school in the Midwest. She asked Felix to come with her, but only if they were a committed couple. Logistically, he could easily move, which actually would enhance his career. Felix realized they couldn't keep repeating the pattern of the past five years. He proposed that they become engaged and move as a committed couple, with the intention of marrying after Claudia completed her first year of medical school. They agreed to approach this move with a view that theirs was a serious, committed relationship that would result in marriage. This was more emotionally wise than "sliding into marriage" because of convenience.

A challenge for Felix and Claudia was to maintain an intimate, erotic relationship without the drama of instability. Sexual desire needs to be nurtured, and the best way to do that in an ongoing relationship is to nurture anticipation and engage in sensual, playful, and erotic touch.

In the past when Felix would get "hard," this was a cue for both of them to go for intercourse. Claudia would avoid touching Felix unless she was receptive to intercourse. The outcome was less touching and less intercourse, and a low-level power struggle ensued that would balloon into a high intensity fight about once a month. Their sexual power struggles resulted in hurt feelings and psychological and relational bruises.

It was Claudia who, while on a walk with Felix, took the initiative to raise the issue of touching options. Claudia missed cuddling (sensual touch) because she couldn't cuddle without Felix getting hard and pushing for intercourse. Felix affirmed that he, too, missed cuddling but missed even more playing around/wrestling (playful touch), which was one of the most engaging aspects of their relationship. Claudia confronted Felix and said that he couldn't have it both ways. They needed to choose. Would they have a variable, flexible sexual relationship with an openness to touch options and outcomes or did arousal demand intercourse? Felix joked, "Can't we have it all?" Claudia countered, "Sometimes yes, sometimes no."

This is the dilemma that confronts couples, whether married or unmarried. They want the freedom of touch options, but also the "naturalness" of intercourse. Like most couples, Claudia and Felix valued intercourse, but Claudia valued sensual and playful touch more than Felix. Claudia felt very good about being orgasmic with manual or oral stimulation while Felix always wanted the "real thing." Rather than allow themselves to remain trapped in a power struggle, Claudia and Felix adopted the "wise" course: They acknowledged that sensuality, playfulness, eroticism, and intercourse were all ways to be sexual—that these four touch dimensions (gears) involve "real sex" by facilitating a sexual connection. With their commitment to marriage and sexuality playing a significant role in relationship vitality and satisfaction, they were able to develop a "win–win" scenario that includes more pleasurable touch and more meaningful intercourse. Claudia and Felix now experience each other as both intimate and erotic friends.

Closing Thoughts

The essence of sexuality is giving and receiving pleasure-oriented touching. The key is to value both verbal (especially outside the bedroom) and nonverbal (especially inside the bedroom) communication and to indulge in a range of sensual, playful, erotic options that often serve as a bridge to intercourse but are valued for themselves. A fundamental basis of your couple sexual style is finding a comfortable way to share sensual, pleasurable, and erotic touch rather than falling into the trap of a pass–fail focus on intercourse performance. Learning about each other's touch gears will help you accept, nurture, and develop your couple sexual style. This is an important step in enriching your sexuality and increasing your satisfaction. In celebrating the everyday joys of loving each other and incorporating all five dimensions of touch into your relationship, you can learn to value a variable, flexible sexuality, which maintains couple vitality and satisfaction.

CHAPTER **4**

Successfully Implementing
Your Couple Sexual Style

Choosing your unique couple sexual style is not a one-time event. It takes most couples six months or longer to transition from the romantic love/passionate sex/idealized phase to develop a mature, intimate couple sexual style. Rather than treating couple sexuality with benign neglect, the challenge is to refine and implement your couple sexual style so that it continues to enhance desire, pleasure, and satisfaction. Even after 10, 20, or even 50 years of a sexual relationship, you can't treat sexuality with benign neglect. If sex is to continue to play an energizing 15–20% role in couple satisfaction, you need to devote emotional and physical energy so your couple sexual style remains vital and satisfying.

Whether you choose the complementary, traditional, soulmate, or emotionally expressive style sketched out in Chapter 2, you both need to acknowledge that decision and commit to making it your own. You want to develop comfort and confidence in your couple sexual style so that sexuality will contribute to relationship vitality and satisfaction. Remember the new mantra of healthy couple sexuality: desire, pleasure, and satisfaction.

You can individualize and refine your core couple style so that it genuinely meets intimacy and sexuality needs. The major challenge is to integrate intimacy and eroticism. Your chosen couple sexual style sets the foundation for how you blend individuality and coupleness and how you integrate a safe and secure intimacy with the specialness and a charge of eroticism. An analogy is purchasing a house in which you plan to live and flourish. The task is to furnish, decorate, and individualize the house so it is truly your own. Choosing a couple sexual style is just the first step in the process. Like furnishing and decorating your house, the following steps will meld increasing individual and relational comfort and confidence with couple sexuality and implement preferences and scenarios that energize your bond and enhance satisfaction.

The process of implementation has two major components. The first is to play to the strengths of your couple sexual style and blend and individualize it so that it genuinely meets individual preferences for intimacy and eroticism and plays a meaningful role in your relationship. Second, learn to be aware of the "traps" of your chosen couple sexual style and ensure that you not fall into these. Your unique couple sexual style can be individualized and implemented in a manner that fits into your real life and feelings, while avoiding the emotional and sexual pitfalls that can interfere with desire, pleasure, and satisfaction.

In reading, discussing, and implementing this material, you need to attend only to the relevant strategies and techniques for your style. You can ignore the material on the other three styles unless you want to increase awareness of diverse strategies and techniques. Knowledge is power. Greater awareness and acceptance promotes healthy individual and couple sexuality.

In his clinical practice, Barry always emphasizes that individual, couple, cultural, and value factors are more important than scientific theory and data when making couple sexual choices. We encourage you to view these materials as guidelines rather than concrete rules. The challenge for you and your mate is to use the information, strategies, techniques, and guidelines to help you implement your unique couple sexual style so that your sexual relationship continues to enhance desire, pleasure, and satisfaction.

Implementing the Complementary Couple Sexual Style

The complementary couple sexual style is the most popular because it is based on each person being responsible for her/his own desire, arousal, and orgasm (discovering your own "sexual voice") while functioning as part of an intimate team to integrate intimacy and eroticism into your relationship. This sexual style balances autonomy and coupleness. Each partner values both intimacy and eroticism. A major strength of this style is the recognition that each partner has a right to his/her sexual preferences, feelings, bridges to desire, preferred pleasuring scenarios, and techniques. Each partner realizes that sex can play different roles and have different meanings at different times, and they enjoy varied afterplay scenarios. The complementary couple accepts that it is normal for each person to initiate and to say no, and that there are many ways to stay connected emotionally and physically.

Equally important is an awareness of typical "traps" of the complementary couple sexual style and a commitment to confront those traps rather than have to dig your way out of them later. Common traps are taking the relationship and sexuality for granted. Sex can fall into a functional but predictable routine so it no longer feels vital and energizing. The birth of a baby and parenting can disrupt the sense of couple equity. Job or house changes can cause frustration and resentment that subvert sexual desire. One partner's emotional or sexual difficulties may lead to avoidance of intimacy rather than turning to the mate as an intimate, erotic friend.

Particularly important in the complementary couple sexual style is that both partners need to be responsible for playing to their strengths and positively influencing their mate. In addition, both must make a commitment to deal with individual, couple, and sexual concerns as a team rather than minimizing issues or falling into a blame/counter-blame trap. An excellent example of individualizing and enhancing your couple sexual style is to be clear about and try out each person's bridges to sexual desire, favorite pleasuring scenarios, favorite ways to experience eroticism, when and how to transition to intercourse, and the afterplay scenario that promotes satisfaction and meaning. A real strength of the complementary couple style is the recognition that each person can enjoy his/her sexual voice and the freedom to play that out. The mate is free to accept, modify, or say this specific technique is not comfortable. The couple does not get trapped in power struggles; instead, the partners work together to affirm a couple sexuality that enhances desires, pleasure, and satisfaction.

Individualizing strengths is a core aspect of the complementary style. Some couples enjoy constructing mutual bridges to desire and mutual erotic scenarios, while other complementary couples emphasize playing to the strengths of each individual's sexual voice with the partner "piggy-backing" on his or her mate's sexual response. For example, the man might have a strong preference for beginning a sexual encounter with playful touching and then switching to erotic dancing. The woman can enjoy his enthusiasm and arousal, but her initiation occurs in the bedroom where she has him read excerpts from *Passionate Hearts* as she touches him. They don't proceed to intercourse until she has been orgasmic with oral stimulation.

Most couples, including those whose sexual style is complementary, prefer finding mutual desire, pleasuring, eroticism, intercourse, and afterplay scenarios. However, the truth is that partners are not clones of each other. Often one partner has preferred bridges to desire, favorite pleasuring techniques and positions, special erotic scenarios, especially satisfying intercourse positions and preferred thrusting rhythms, and enjoys different ways of savoring afterplay. More than any other couple style, the complementary couple is open to and can accept these divergent preferences and scenarios.

In individualizing your complementary couple sexual style, a crucial element is to ensure that you add new scenarios rather than settle into a complacent routine. This is especially true when there is a change in life circumstances (birth of a baby, recovery from a health or economic setback, transition to retirement). Complementary couples take pride in the equity and flexibility of their couple sexuality. However, you cannot treat this relationship as a "done deal" and become complacent. You need to put new energy into refining your sexual style.

A helpful strategy adopted by many complementary couples is that one partner agrees to initiate a new element during a six-month period, while in the next six months the other partner takes the initiative to introduce sexual innovations. This facilitates playing to the strength of your couple sexual style and serves to maintain sexual freshness and vitality. The initiative can be something as minor as trying a new lotion or pleasuring position or something as major as establishing a tradition of a weekend away without the children each year or trying a role enactment arousal scenario that is "politically incorrect" such as master–slave.

The reason that the complementary couple sexual style is the most popular is that it emphasizes the importance of each partner having a sexual voice and working together as an intimate sexual team. Play to the strengths of your couple sexual style by emphasizing individual sexual preferences and requests, so you maintain sexual vitality and variability. Be aware of the traps of resting on your laurels and losing your sense of sexual equity. If loss of sexual vitality begins, confront this as an intimate team and attitudinally, behaviorally, and emotionally acknowledge your personal and couple commitment to renew desire, pleasure, and satisfaction.

Implementing the Traditional Couple Sexual Style

This second most common couple sexual style has very powerful factors that facilitate its success and satisfaction. In implementing your chosen couple style, be aware that the traditional couple sexual style is the most predictable and, stable sexual style, allowing partners to enjoy freedom from anxiety and insecurity. In this style couples value the intimacy and security associated with stable marriages, as well as enjoy the support of extended family, religion, and community. Conflict-minimizing couples are typically very child- and family-oriented, which adds a special dimension and meaning to their lives. Many couples say sex was best in their marriage when they were trying to get pregnant and reaping the joys of sharing intercourse and conception.

An important strength to play to in the traditional style is recognition and enjoyment of complementary aspects of traditional gender roles. The female initiates affectionate touch and emphasizes the value of emotional intimacy. The male initiates sex and emphasizes the role and meaning of sexual intercourse in their lives and marriage. Sex is viewed as a natural part of marriage, not a source of conflict requiring conversation and negotiation.

In individualizing and implementing your traditional couple sexual style, the question is what can each of you do to enhance the strengths. For example, would a regular couple date night followed by a sexual experience enhance sexual anticipation? Would the man introducing an alternative intercourse position or switching positions during intercourse enhance couple sexual satisfaction? Would the woman introducing a new afterplay scenario centered on increased emotional bonding enhance the meaning of sex for the couple? Would affirming the energizing role of marital sex solidify your husband–wife bond?

Both a strength and vulnerability of the traditional sexual style is that the partners find it easiest to accept becoming a non-sexual couple. The conflict-minimizing couple does not want strong negative emotions or drama to disrupt their lives and relationship, so they can more easily accept the cessation of intercourse, especially if they continue an affectionate and emotional connection. The vulnerability for this couple sexual style is that the non-sexual relationship is a loss for the man, the woman, and the couple. Special feelings of desire and energy are missing. They've lost the positive 15–20% sexual resource. The good thing is they don't allow a non-sexual marriage to degenerate into an attack–counterattack dynamic that results in emotional and relational alienation.

The two major traps of the traditional couple sexual style are losing a genuine sense of intimate connection and the inability to deal with unexpected relational and sexual realities. In implementing your chosen couple sexual style, you need to ensure that you do not fall into these traps. The first vulnerability is the easiest to prevent, and you don't need to make a major modification to your couple style to do so. Some couples individualize their traditional sexual style by having the woman initiate at least a quarter of the sexual experiences. Or once a month she might initiate her special intimacy/pleasuring/intercourse scenario, which is energizing for her and for them as a couple. Other couples make certain that the woman (at least on occasion) chooses when to transition to intercourse and guides intromission. Other interventions are for the man to initiate a sensual massage to reinforce the value of sharing pleasure with no demand for intercourse or orgasm. Another example is to have in-laws or siblings watch the children for a day so the partners can go on a hike, antiquing, to lunch, visit with friends, go to a museum, or catch a movie so they have special time as a couple.

Bad things happen to good people and couples. Whether it is dealing with an infertility problem, an affair, erectile dysfunction, or a depression causing inhibited sexual desire, even the most traditional and religious couples experience difficult sexual issues. A key factor is to accept the difficult sexual reality rather than pretend it isn't true or avoid talking about the problem. It is important not to fall into the guilt/blame trap or feel this is God's punishment. God wants you to be a healthy sexual person and a healthy sexual couple, not to to be self-punitive or punish your partner.

Ideally, the best strategy is prevention. For example, realize that infertility is a medical issue, not a moral issue. Use all your resources to address it: choose an infertility specialist, increase your knowledge of treatment options, join a support group. Most of all, realize this will be very stressful on your sexual relationship, especially if you do not approach this as an intimate team. Affairs can occur in a good marriage where there is healthy sex and adherence to traditional religious values. The best affair prevention program is an awareness of vulnerable moods, people, and situations. Share these concerns with your spouse and agree to talk about the risk before the affair becomes reality. If an affair or incidence of unfaithfulness has occurred, disclose it within a week. Affairs thrive on secrecy and, just as in politics, the cover-up is worse than the reality. Remember, 70% of couples can and do survive affairs.

The second strategy is to deal with the problem and promote healing. Don't play the "if only" game. You can learn from the past, but you cannot change the past. Acknowledging that the problem exists is not the same as condoning it or forgetting about it. Accepting the reality of an infertility problem, an affair, or sexual alienation is a crucial step in approaching the problem as a challenge for you as a couple. The goal is a return to a comfortable sexual equilibrium. An even greater challenge is to build a more comfortable, functional, traditional couple sexual style. The most crucial lession to be learned from the crisis is to not take couple sexuality for granted; instead, devote time and attention to keeping intimacy and sexuality alive in your marriage.

Another modification of the traditional style might entail decreasing the rigidity of gender roles and emphasizing flexibility and sharing of intimacy and eroticism by both spouses. An additional resource is to create an early warning signal for intimacy and sexuality problems and deal with them in the acute stage rather than waiting until there is a crisis.

Traditional couples, as well as adherents of other couple styles, need to play to the strengths of their chosen style, while being aware of and monitoring potential traps of this style so they do not subvert sexual satisfaction.

Implementing the Soulmate Couple Sexual Style

Traditionally, the soulmate couple sexual style was viewed as the superior choice. The more intimacy, the better. Being sexual with a partner who totally knew and loved you was the ideal. Acceptance and security was expected to be very high.

Couples who choose this style in an aware, affirmative manner enhance relationship intimacy and security. Sharing intimacy and eroticism with your soulmate can be highly satisfying. In implementing this style, it is crucial to be sure that your mutual level of intimacy facilitates feeling erotic with each other; emotional closeness cannot be allowed to smother eroticism. Also, ensure that pleasurable touch is playful and that you can express and enjoy a range of ways to connect emotionally and sexually.

Rather than being totally dependent on partner interaction arousal, some soulmate couples purposefully utilize role enactment arousal scenarios to spice up their sexual repertoire and introduce mystery and eroticism to their relationship. They might also be open to one-way erotic scenarios to supplement the focus on couple equity. Another technique is to encourage each spouse to be "sexually selfish" once a month and introduce a highly personal erotic scenario. In playing to the strengths of your soulmate couple sexual style, be sure you savor sharing your emotions and sexuality without fear of criticalness or judgment. Share affectionate, sensual, playful, erotic, and intercourse touch and realize that the best aphrodisiac is an involved, aroused partner.

Soulmate sexual couples are open to sharing both positive and negative emotions, as well as open to negative sexual feedback and requests for change. To make this a personal and concrete part of your soulmate style, you could purposefully set aside time every six months to share a negative feeling or behavior and make a request for change. A key factor in implementing your soulmate couple sexual style is to emphasize the positive influence process, especially in terms of eroticism.

Being aware of potential traps of the soulmate couple sexual style is particularly important. This couple style is vulnerable to three major traps. The first is disappointment/disillusion, especially on the woman's part, about the partner and relationship, leading to inhibited sexual desire. The second is de-eroticizing the partner. The third is the inability to recover from negative intimate or sexual experiences, especially an affair.

Awareness and prevention is the most effective strategy. In terms of the first trap, do not idealize your partner or relationship. Putting your partner on a pedestal almost guarantees a hard fall and a painful breaking of your intimate bond. Be sure you chose the soulmate couple sexual style for positive reasons rather than because that's what your friends, family, religion, or media said you "should" do. Be aware of each person's emotional and sexual vulnerabilities rather than believing love will resolve everything. We believe in positive, realistic couple expectations, not idealistic standards or the "magic of love." Establish a balance between intimacy and eroticism. You don't want so much intimacy that it shuts off eroticism, i.e., feeling so close that there's no space for erotic scenarios and techniques.

Affairs occur in the most loving, sexually functional relationships. We discourage affairs, but you need to deal with the reality of an affair and learn from the experience by processing it. This allows you to develop a coherent meaning for the involved partner, the injured partner, and the relationship. Soulmate couples have a hard time following these guidelines. They become stuck in the blame/guilt trap and never rebuild couple trust and sexuality. Rather than the couple dealing with the affair, the affair controls the relationship and couple sexuality. If this is the case, we strongly urge you to seek resources from Appendix A to deal with the aftermath of an affair in a therapeutic manner.

The soulmate couple sexual style is no longer viewed as the ideal because it requires so much thought and effort to implement successfully. In addition, it contains a number of traps that can subvert eroticism and sexuality. However, if this is your chosen couple sexual style we strongly urge you to acknowledge the very real strengths of this style, individualize it to attain a healthy balance of intimacy and eroticism, and be especially aware and vigilant so you avoid common traps.

Implementing the Emotionally Expressive Couple Sexual Style

This couple sexual style is the most exciting and erotic, and is envied by other couples. Emotionally expressive couples experience more vitality, fun, and genuine celebration of the joys of sex than those of any other couple style. In addition, it is the most flexible and resilient couple sexual style. This "fun and erotic" style is wonderful when it works well, but it is the least stable couple style, especially in terms of relational security and longevity. How can you implement your chosen emotionally expressive couple sexual style so that it truly plays to your strengths and avoids the common traps?

A genuine strength of this sexual style is that it emphasizes eroticism and taking emotional and sexual risks. Emotionally expressive couples are particularly open to partner interaction arousal and role enactment arousal. They clearly and strongly express emotions—both positive and negative. These couples use sex to heal from conflict and value sexual resiliency. Of all couple styles, the emotionally expressive couple can most readily recover from an affair: They yell, cry, and are sexual.

In implementing this couple sexual style, what are the specific ways for you to enhance sexual vitality and satisfaction? For example, you can organize a trip to a sex shop or go online to purchase sex toys or videos to provide a special erotic charge. Some couples focus on the other end of the continuum—how to ensure that their intimate bond remains resilient and secure. These couples use afterplay scenarios that emphasize savoring erotic experiences or acknowledging the value of their intimacy/eroticism balance. Still other couples enjoy experimenting with scenarios in which one partner sexually "does" the mate and asks nothing in return. A common erotic scenario is to be sexual in "forbidden places"—on a beach, in your office, on an overnight plane, in your backyard on a warm night at 3 a.m., in your parents' bedroom. Focus on the creativity and joy of your chosen couple sexual style.

What are the potential traps of the emotionally expressive couple sexual style? The two main ones are breaking personal boundaries and emotionally wearing each other out. Strengths of a couple sexual style when taken to an extreme can become a fatal flaw. Clear, genuine, emotionally charged communication can increase vitality, but when it becomes a personal attack on the partner, especially the partner's sexuality, it can be devastating. Angry fights during or after a negative sexual encounter are destructive, controlled by hurt, impulsivity, and anger that cause "hit-below-the-belt" accusations. There is something about lying in bed nude after a negative sexual experience that makes a person feel very vulnerable and can bring out the worst in the couple. Whether intentional or not, impulsive sexual put-downs subvert intimacy and trust.

Resilience is a strength of the emotionally expressive couple sexual style, but it is negated by the strain of recovering from the fifth affair or encounters that continually break down into sexual attacks and counterattacks. In essence, the emotionally expressive couple sexual style buckles under the frequency and intensity of sexual dramas.

In implementing your chosen couple style it is crucial to respect personal and sexual boundaries and not wear out your partner or relationship. We encourage each partner to list three to five emotional or sexual "poisons" that the mate agrees to refrain from no matter what. In addition, the partners should agree to back off when one partner signals being overwhelmed by the emotional intensity. Emotionally expressive partners need to be especially aware not to use sex as a way to hurt their mate. You genuinely want to enjoy the vitality and intensity of your couple sexual style and protect it against "poisons."

Closing Thoughts

As you individualize your unique couple sexual style, play to the strengths of your chosen style while being aware of and monitoring traps. This ensures that your couple sexuality continues to promote desire, pleasure, and satisfaction. With the aging of the partners and the relationship, it is healthy to modify and refine elements that facilitate valuing and enjoying your unique couple sexual style. The great majority of couples acknowledge the benefits of their chosen sexual style, especially when it is flexible enough to incorporate individual preferences and changes in life circumstances. The couples who do change their sexual style are most likely to adopt the complementary sexual style because of its emphasis on each partner's own sexual voice while functioning as an intimate team.

As you proceed through the concepts, guidelines, and exercises in this book be aware of your chosen couple sexual style and implement relevant strategies and techniques so that sexuality continues to contribute 15–20% to couple vitality and satisfaction.

PART II

Enhancing Desire and Satisfaction

CHAPTER 5

Keeping Your Sexual Options Open

Traditionally, sex therapy focused on intercourse and orgasm. The new mantra for healthy couple sexuality is desire, pleasure, and satisfaction. Intercourse and orgasm are positive, integral components of couple sexuality. However, focusing solely on intercourse and orgasm diverts you from the best sexual experiences. Couples who develop a satisfying sexuality enhance desire, share pleasure, savor eroticism, and feel energized, bonded, and satisfied. This is true whether or not the sexual experience was "great" and even when the sex did not involve mutuality. Of course, the most satisfying sexual encounters involve desire, arousal, orgasm, and satisfaction for both partners. But wise couples realize that even "okay" sexual experiences are worthwhile.

Healthy couples nurture sexual desire as the core element in their sexuality. They are not embarrassed or worried that often one (usually the man) is more desirous than the other or that one partner's desire (usually that of the woman) is responsive to touch or emotional needs rather than experiencing spontaneous desire. The important factor is that each person anticipates and feels deserving of a satisfying sexuality and accepts that there is a range of ways to connect physically and emotionally, a range of bridges to desire, and a range of dimensions and meanings to the sexual experience.

The most common connotation of sex is a shared pleasure. In addition, sex can be a way to reestablish or deepen intimacy, as well as a tension reducer to deal with external stresses or the hassles inherent in sharing your lives. It can reaffirm desirability and self-esteem, and at times fulfill the traditional biological purpose of conceiving a child. Wise couples realize it is not only normal, but healthy, to have different intimacy agendas, just as it's healthy to have different bridges to sexual desire. Your couple sexual style can nurture a vital, resilient sexual desire.

The essence of sexuality is giving and receiving pleasure-oriented touching. Pleasuring is very different than foreplay, where the man stimulates the woman to get her ready for intercourse. In contrast, pleasuring involves giving and receiving touch to facilitate sexual receptivity and response. Of course, developing an erotic flow that leads to intercourse is a welcome outcome, but it is not a performance demand. Pleasuring involves sensual, playful, and erotic non-intercourse (manual, oral, rubbing) touch. Each phase of non-demand pleasuring has value in itself, as well as the possibility of serving as a bridge to greater arousal and intercourse. Touching inside and outside the bedroom without the demand for intercourse is a wonderful way for partners to share intimacy and pleasure.

What is the essence of satisfaction? It is the acceptance of yourself and your partner as intimate, sexual beings. Satisfaction requires neither orgasm nor mutuality, although both orgasm and mutuality are highly valued couple experiences. The integration of emotional and sexual satisfaction is optimal, but you can experience emotional satisfaction in a number of non-optimal situations, including feeling close and warm even though non-orgasmic, enjoying your partner's arousal and orgasm, enjoying being the giving partner, experiencing intimate or light-hearted afterplay to enhance bonding, trying a different erotic scenario, and feeling you are growing as a sexual person and as a couple.

Is it possible to feel physical satisfaction even if orgasm does not occur? Traditionally, women have said yes and men have said no. In fact, for both women and men, sensuality and playful touch can be physically satisfying. If one or both partners feel sexually "turned-on" (including intercourse), can one or both experience physical satisfaction without orgasm? Do not give a "politically correct" answer. This is a crucially important question for your sexual relationship.

A sexual encounter that flows from comfort to pleasure to arousal to the erotic to intercourse to orgasm is optimal both physically and emotionally. Orgasm, for either partner, whether during intercourse or with manual, oral, rubbing, or vibrator stimulation, is physically satisfying. It is crucial to recognize that individuals and couples have different arousal/orgasm preferences, and different meanings for orgasm. Some regard it as a tension reliever, while others view it as an intense erotic experience or as the natural result of an intimate encounter. Orgasm has a different meaning in one-way sex as opposed to mutual sex, or as the culmination of a two-minute "quickie" as opposed to a two-hour lovemaking scenario.

The most important fact you can learn about your couple sexual style is that satisfaction (both physical and emotional) does not require orgasm. Sometimes a non-orgasmic experience can be highly satisfying (for the man as well as the woman) while at other times an orgasmic experience is dissatisfying for the man, the woman, or the couple. The broader, more flexible, and more variable the couple's acceptance and satisfaction, the better for your emotional and sexual health.

Chris and Nathan This was 37-year-old Chris's second marriage and 41-year-old Nathan's first. The two children from Chris's first marriage were 16 and 14. Chris realized that step-parenting two adolescent children was not going to be easy for Nathan, and they hoped that sex would be a "port in the storm" as they adapted to being a four-person family. The biological father had been involved with the children after the divorce, but six years ago he had remarried, moved out of state, and begun a second family. Since then his emotional and financial involvement with the children had been minimal.

Nathan realized that loving Chris was not enough. He had to accept her children as part of the whole package. Children of that age are not looking for a substitute father, but they did accept Nathan in a favorite uncle role. Nathan did not try to be the disciplinarian or "heavy." Having two adolescent children at home can have a negative impact on the most loving sexual couple. Chris and Nathan realized it would be an important challenge to create their couple sexual style—which they very much wanted to achieve.

Nathan brought significant strengths to the marriage but also significant vulnerabilities, especially his attitudes about intimate sexuality. Although he had not been married before, Nathan had had a number of relationships, including three cohabiting relationships. For Nathan, sex was more exciting and erotic at the beginning of the relationship. Although he'd had a three- and five-year relationship as well as three two-year relationships (a pattern of serial monogamy), sexual desire and vitality waned and was usually gone by the time the relationship ended. When Nathan started a new relationship, he experienced renewed desire. Maintaining desire, pleasure, and satisfaction in a stable relationship was not in Nathan's life experience.

Chris also brought considerable strengths as well as vulnerabilities to this marriage. She had been a good single mother and a well-organized human resources professional. An optimistic, extroverted person, Chris was committed to having a successful second marriage and four-person family. Her two biggest vulnerabilities were that although she liked and respected Nathan, she didn't understand his emotional and sexual vulnerabilities. The second vulnerability was that Chris saw sex as the man's domain, not hers.

Unfortunately, after less than a year of marriage, sex was both infrequent and low quality. Each felt resentful and blamed for the sexual problem. Chris had undergone a tubal sterilization before meeting Nathan so contraception wasn't an issue. Chris could not understand why even though she offered to be sexual during stressful times Nathan didn't seem particularly interested; nor was he satisfied when they had sex. Was he not attracted to her, had he fallen out of love, or was she just not good enough sexually?

The optimal way to approach a sexual issue is for each person to take responsibility for her/his sexuality and then work together as an intimate team to develop a comfortable, functional couple sexual style. For Chris and Nathan this meant talking about sexuality on their daily morning walks and when in their bedroom to confront the avoidance pattern and physically move toward each other. This involved Chris finding her own sexual voice rather than waiting to react to Nathan's initiations and pre-ferred sexual scenario. For Nathan, it meant stepping up to the challenge of integrating intimacy and eroticism into marital sex.

Chris and Nathan agreed to split the week. Chris took from Sunday at noon to Thursday evening, and Nathan had Friday morning until Sunday noon. Each person volunteered to initiate a sexual encounter during their time of the week. Once Chris got over her self-consciousness she was very enthusiastic about initiating. She particularly enjoyed planning encounters when the children were out of the house. Chris talked Nathan into going to work later on some mornings. They would take a walk and she would share with him the sexual scenario she wanted to try. After the kids were off to school, Chris and Nathan would play sexually.

Chris had always settled for partner interaction arousal scenarios in which she responded to her partner's foreplay. Now Chris experimented with mutual pleasuring scenarios, taking the lead and setting the pace of sensual and playful touching, choosing when to transition to genital/erotic stimulation, and initiating guided intromission when she was feeling highly aroused. Chris also introduced role enactment arousal scenarios. One morning she dressed in a Victoria's Secret outfit and did a striptease for Nathan. The next week she asked him to dress in his sexiest outfit and do a strip for her. Her favorite scenario was Nathan reading aloud a pas-sage from a "steamy" novel as she seductively touched him while he con-tinued reading.

Nathan's initiations and bridges to desire were quite different than Chris's. Sometimes this is a struggle for couples, but Chris and Nathan were receptive to each others' bridges to desire. Nathan liked to surprise Chris, making his initiation particularly inviting. Nathan realized he needed to actively nurture desire and be creative to maintain his desire for a vital marital sexuality.

For Chris and Nathan, having different arousal styles and erotic scenar-ios facilitated desire. Chris emphasized the concept of non-demand plea-suring more enthusiastically than Nathan, but he realized that touching outside the bedroom was good for their relationship and promoted desire and flexible couple sexuality. The biggest divide between Nathan and Chris was their approach to orgasm and satisfaction. Chris was more orgasmic than ever in her life. She enjoyed being orgasmic with both manual and intercourse stimulation. On occasion, she enjoyed cunnilingus as a pleasuring technique, but not to orgasm. Chris was orgasmic in more than 85% of couple encounters (which she assured Nathan was higher than average for women). Nathan was orgasmic in over 99% of encounters and was frustrated on the rare occasions when he wasn't. On several occasions, Chris found a non-orgasmic experience more satisfying than those in which she had to work hard to be orgasmic.

The other scenario that confused Nathan was that Chris found one-way giving (manual and oral sex) much more pleasurable and satisfying than intercourse when she was not feeling sexual. Chris told Nathan not to feel embarrassed or selfish. This was a satisfying emotional experience for her. She really enjoyed seeing his heightened arousal and orgasm. Couples who value a variable, flexible desire/pleasure/satisfaction style have a major marital resource.

Increase Pleasure by Being Open and Flexible

The woman becomes aware that it is her passion that increases his desire and the man discovers that it is his openness to a range of sensual and sexual experiences that increases the frequency and intensity of couple sexuality. The man's obsessive focus on intercourse frequency and orgasm and the woman's primary focus on intimacy and sensuality set up an unnecessary power struggle. In truth, individuals and couples are different than cultural/gender stereotypes. Many women enjoy spontaneous and passionate sexual encounters. We've been surprised by the number of women who value role enactment arousal scenarios that focus on eroticism and downplay intimacy. Likewise, the number of males who enjoy sharing a Jacuzzi or hot tub is surprising. It is interesting how much more comfortable men are giving back rubs than receiving, but when they are open to receiving they report reveling in the sensuality. Individually and as a couple there is greater desire, pleasure, and satisfaction when there is greater openness and flexibility in gender roles.

Exercise: Finding Your Desire, Pleasure, Satisfaction Style

You can implement an approach to desire, pleasure, and satisfaction that brings out the best in you as a person and as a couple. The essence of desire is positive anticipation and feeling you deserve pleasure in your relationship. The more ways to cue desire the better, as is the realization that it is normal and healthy for you and your partner to experience desire in different ways at different times. Identify at least two and up to five ways to facilitate desire, and share all but one with your partner. (It's good to keep some mystery in your sex life.)

The core of sexuality is giving and receiving pleasure-oriented touching. Pleasurable touch can be done inside and outside the bedroom, clothed and unclothed, in a sensual and playful manner, including genital and non-genital contact. Tell your partner your favorite ways to share pleasure and, even more important, play out two or more pleasuring scenarios.

Satisfaction includes openness to orgasm, but is much more than orgasm. To make this personal and concrete, we encourage you to share with your partner your favorite afterplay scenario. What are the emotional and physical experiences that allow you to feel especially close or energized after a sexual encounter?

The next phase of this exercise is to talk outside of the bedroom— whether on a walk or over a glass of wine or cup of tea—about your new sexual mantra of desire, pleasure, and satisfaction. How is it different for you than the old approach that focused on sexual performance based on intercourse and orgasm? How can you integrate this new mantra into your couple sexual style so that your sexual relationship grows stronger and more resilient as you age?

Closing Thoughts

The new sexual mantra of desire, pleasure, and satisfaction is a core resource for establishing a strong, resilient couple sexual style. Intercourse and orgasm are integral components of couple sexuality, but your sexuality is not hostage to sexual performance. Individual and couple sexuality has room to breathe, grow, and be flexible when you are open to a myriad of ways to create and nurture desire, emphasize sexuality as sharing pleasure, and enjoy yourselves emotionally and sexually. These experiences can enhance emotional and sexual satisfaction. Satisfaction is not tied to orgasm; nor is it lost because orgasm does not occur during a sensual, playful, or erotic encounter. Focusing on performance and the goal of orgasm limits your sexuality. Enjoy the many pleasures and satisfaction of touching, sensuality, pleasuring, and eroticism that facilitate but do not depend on intercourse.

CHAPTER **6**

Building Bridges to Desire

In movies desire is spontaneous and natural; the couple is turned-on and ready to go. There is no need for touching. The big screen offers up a powerful, seductive model that frankly has little relevance for your couple sexual style. The truth for real-life couples (especially those with jobs, kids, and house responsibilities) is that sexual desire involves finding personally inviting ways to anticipate and initiate sex. More than 80% of sexual encounters are planned or semi-planned, although spontaneous sex is particularly fun and valued. Most important, touch is integral to desire rather than desire spontaneously appearing.

The key is to develop "his," "her," and "our" bridges to sexual desire. These bridges can be intimate, erotic, or both. The more varied and frequent the bridges, the more likely you will have a satisfying sexual relationship. Desire is the core sexual component, and inhibited sexual desire is the major couple sexual problem. Among couples entering sex therapy, 80% complain of desire problems.

There are as many causes of desire problems as there are couples. The most common cause is that the couple never transitioned from the romantic love/passionate sex/idealization phase (which usually lasts between six months and two years—three years at the most) to developing an intimate, erotic couple sexual style. The cultural myth is that sexual desire is magic. In reality, desire is multi-causal, complex, and variable. It can be facilitated, or it can be subverted. A key is to integrate intimacy (a sense of closeness, safety, predictability) with eroticism (taking personal and sexual risks, creating fantasy and mystery, experiencing emotionally and sexually charged unpredictability). A loss of intimacy and loving feelings will ultimately steal sex away. The other extreme of too much closeness and intimacy leaves no space to share sexual playfulness, and you de-eroticize your partner.

Our concept of bridges to desire helps focus you in a personally inviting manner on ways to anticipate being sexual. This can include touch, fantasy, seductive talk, sexual dates, or using role-enactment stimuli such as X-rated videos, sex toys, or sex games. For many couples the main bridge to sexual desire is talking and touching, perhaps over a glass of wine in the family room or on the deck. They do not transition to the bedroom until they are already turned on. For other couples it is getting out of their house, going to dinner, a concert, or a comedy club and feeling emotionally playful and receptive before they get home. Still other couples take a shower or bath together while engaging in sex play or read love poems or erotic stories to set a mood. Some use sexual desire as a playful way to wake up after a nap, to reconnect after being apart for a week on business travel or to make up after an argument.

Sexual desire can serve a number of personal and couple needs. It is normal and healthy for each person's sexual agenda to be different. Sometimes sexual desire is driven by a need for tension reduction, other times to share pleasure, at times to reconnect after a period of alienation or soothe disappointment after a job setback. Sometimes sex celebrates a joyful event such as a birthday or anniversary, recognizes the delivery of an antique desk you coveted, offers hope of conceiving a baby, starts a weekend or vacation. Sex can be a way to break out of mild depressive feelings, offer a "port in the storm" after a stressful encounter with your teenager, or facilitate sleep. The function and role of sexual desire is varied and multidimensional.

This is also true with bridges to sexual desire. Sometimes the bridge is intentional, with one partner saying, "I want to make love." At other times it can be a non-verbal cue such as brushing your teeth and showering. More often, the sexual encounter evolves from "playing around." With receptivity and responsivity to touch sexual desire is ignited. Unexpected, spontaneous sexual encounters are particularly valued for demonstrating genuine loving feelings. But we believe planned, semi-structured bridges to desire are just as genuine and express awareness of the psychological, relational, and sexual need to maintain couple sexual vitality.

Susan and Bill   Susan and Bill met as 20-year-olds in a college creative writing class. They were both dating other people, so their relationship started as a friendship with a focus on supporting each other's writing and creativity. Bill was supportive when during senior year Susan chose to take the LSAT and apply to law school. Her boyfriend was not supportive. He wanted Susan to accompany him to his country of origin and support his career. This conflict eventually broke up their relationship, and Bill was very eager to turn his friendship with Susan into a romantic/sexual relationship. The first four months of their sexual relationship was "dynamite." Starting as friends can serve as a very special launching pad for an erotic relationship, as long as there is mutual attraction. It is the romantic love/passionate sex/idealization that allows people to take the risk and invest in a new relationship. Bill and Susan recall their first four months as a romantic sexual couple very fondly. When they experience periods of frustration or stagnation, they remember those times, and it softens their relational agitation.

The initial phase of a sexual relationship is all about spontaneous desire, being sexual almost every time you are together, with the focus on partner interaction and arousal. Bill and Susan were psychologically and sexually sophisticated and realized that their couple sexual style needed to evolve. They wanted to develop a mature, intimate, interactive couple style (and not compare it to the first four months). They didn't want to fall into the traditional gender traps of Bill valuing frequency and eroticism and Susan valuing lovemaking quality with a sole emphasis on intimacy. Both Bill and Susan learned to value intimacy, pleasuring, and eroticism. The key to building bridges to desire is for partners to anticipate a sexual encounter. Both partners must value couple sex and feel they deserve sexuality to play a positive role in relationship vitality and satisfaction.

Susan wanted to have "her" bridges to desire, Bill to have "his" bridges, and together develop "their" bridges. Over the next 3 years (19 months as a married couple), they developed favorite ways to keep desire alive and initiate sexual encounters. Bill particularly liked spontaneous, erotic encounters while Susan most enjoyed a sexual experience in the context of sharing time and feelings. They did not allow this to break down into rigid gender stereotypes. Susan could initiate a "quickie" as a tension reducer, and Bill could enjoy a couple evening of listening to music and sharing emotions before or after a sexual encounter.

Susan's favorite bridges to desire were taking a bath together, having a glass of wine while listening to classical music, spending a lot of time with oral sex before transitioning to intercourse, and having breakfast in bed and lingering over coffee while reading romantic poems from *Passionate Hearts*. She enjoyed having Bill be the sexually giving partner and turning to sex with Bill as a "port in the storm" after a stressful day at work to reenergize her sense of worth and serve as a reminder of the value of their shared life.

Bill had very different bridges to desire. By far his favorite was taking a shower in the morning and coming back to bed, where Susan manually and orally pleasured him before switching to energetic intercourse that involved giving and receiving multiple stimulation. He liked when Susan woke him up in the middle of the night by stroking his penis and kissing him, and putting him inside of her. After going with friends to a musical or sporting event, he enjoyed leaving early, playing in the car, and being highly turned on before arriving in the bedroom.

Susan and Bill had two shared bridges—one traditional and the other their special bridge. The traditional mutual bridge was going to an early movie (often a romantic comedy), then to their favorite tapas wine bar for a light gourmet meal, and home for sex. Their special bridge involved technology and role enactment arousal. Both loved the new communication technology and used it to build sexual anticipation. They pretended not to know each other, and Susan was ambivalent about meeting for a hook-up. They would leave voice mails, e-mails, "IM" each other as Bill tried to seduce Susan to meet him for sex. It was both a playful and erotic way to anticipate a sexual date.

Susan and Bill were committed to having a satisfying, stable marriage in which intimacy and sexuality played a 15–20% role in maintaining relational vitality. They would not take their sexual relationship for granted. Continuing to experiment with ways to initiate a sexual encounter added a special dimension to their couple sexual style.

The Dangers of "Politically Correct" Desire

Love songs and R-rated movies present a very inviting and seductive approach to sexual desire. Love, longing, and lust happen during each song and with each on-screen encounter. This can be sexually titillating; it's only a problem if this approach is treated as the only "right" way to initiate sex.

On the other extreme, being "politically correct" kills eroticism. Demanding emotional and sexual mutuality kills desire. Self-consciously asking if the partner feels receptive to sex can squelch an opportunity. The truth of sexual desire is that it is not politically correct. Sometimes desire is unilateral; sometimes it involves a biological drive for a tension-reducing orgasm rather than a loving feeling; sometimes it's about opportunity, while at other times it's an emotional gift. Sometimes desire is selfish, sometimes cued by external stimuli and fantasy having nothing to do with your partner, while at other times it's a sexual power play. If all sexual desire and expression had to be loving and mutual, you would cut sexual frequency by at least 70%. If you accept that there are many personal and couple bridges to sexual desire, as least half of which are not politically correct, you will have a much richer and satisfying sexual life.

Exercise: Creating Your Special Bridges—His, Hers, and Ours

The concepts and case study in this chapter offer a smorgasbord of bridges and techniques to anticipate sexuality and initiate a sexual encounter, but it will only be valuable for you if you actually make it personal and concrete by developing your own individual and couple bridges. We suggest using your most comfortable way to communicate with your partner (face-to-face conversation, on a walk, while folding laundry, via e-mail, letter, or phone). Tell him/her your two favorite ways to initiate a sexual encounter and your two favorite ways to be invited for a sexual encounter.

Don't turn this into a sterile, step-by-step process (sex is not like a detailed cooking recipe). However, you do need to be clear about your favorite ways to start an encounter and the most personally inviting ways for your partner to initiate one. Most people find it quite easy to say what they don't want or like; the real emotional and sexual challenge is to verbalize the inviting bridges that facilitate anticipation and openness. For you, what is the right mix of verbal/non-verbal, intentional/playful, indirect/direct, intimate/erotic, and seductive/explicit ways to reach out for a sexual experience?

Just as important is determining how to say no and offer an alternative or ask for a raincheck. It's only in the movies that the answer is always yes and sex flows easily. Real-life couples often say no. They are busy, distracted, tired, want to do something else, or are just not up for sex. How do you convey this so that your partner doesn't feel rejected or put down? How do you offer an option that could be affectionate, sensual, playful, or mutually or one-way erotic? How do you stay positive and connected when you don't want to have intercourse? You can't genuinely say yes to sex unless you can comfortably say "no." This is a core concept. Remember, bridges to desire are requests, not demands.

Having "our" mutual bridges to desire is a powerful couple resource. Some couples develop simple mutual bridges. They enjoy getting into pajamas after the children are in bed, cuddle, have a beer, touch while watching a DVD, and turn the DVD off to go to the bedroom when they feel turned on. These same couples often have special, complex scenarios—a Saturday night date or waking to a playful touch after an afternoon nap. A special bridge might involve going to an early movie; as he drives the babysitter home she makes a light appetizer, pours a glass of wine, lights a scented candle, and puts on their favorite CD. When he returns instead of jumping into sex, he is open to connecting and playing, which could include a slow, sensual massage or reading aloud from his favorite love poem. She could surprise him with an erotic outfit and playful dance or set a scenario in which her arousal leads his.

"Our" bridges to desire are a couple challenge; they ask you to develop mutual ways to connect and initiate desire. What is your special way to create scenarios? Do you talk over the dinner table or play it out in the bedroom? Do you have predictable bridges or special bridges? Is your emphasis on intimacy or eroticism or on partner interaction, self-entracement, or role enactment scenarios? You owe it to yourself, each other, and your sexual relationship to develop comfortable, inviting mutual bridges to sexual desire. These should be in addition to, not instead of, each partner's individual bridges to desire.

Planned and Spontaneous Bridges

Romantic spontaneous bridges to sexual desire are almost every couple's first preference. Let us be clear: Spontaneous sexual desire is very special and energizing. When it happens, allow yourself to really enjoy it. However, be aware that even for the most loving, satisfied couples, 80% of sexual encounters are planned or semi-planned. With jobs, children, household chores, and social and community responsibilities claiming our time, that is the truth for the great majority of couples who have been together two years or longer.

Bridges to desire require ways of thinking, anticipating, and experiencing a sexual encounter that makes sex inviting. Anticipation is the most important bridge. For example, if you have a sexual daydream or see an attractive person at the coffee shop, allow that image to "simmer" throughout the day so it serves as a bridge for sexual initiation that evening. Erotic cues and scenarios facilitate anticipation and desire. Planned sexual dates are particularly important in maintaining sexual vitality. The most powerful bridge is anticipating an encounter in which the partner is involved, giving, and aroused. The more varied the bridges, the easier it is to maintain desire.

Closing Thoughts

Developing and maintaining sexual desire is crucial to your couple sexual style. Desire is the core element in healthy sexuality. The more bridges to desire, the more ways to connect and reconnect through touch. Touching, which occurs both inside and outside the bedroom, is a prime way to maintain desire. Not all touching can or should lead to intercourse. Touching is a way to stay connected and serves as a bridge to desire, pleasure, and eroticism. Valuing both intimacy and eroticism and enjoying both planned and spontaneous sexual experiences produces stronger and more resilient couple sexuality.

CHAPTER 7

Indulging in Eroticism and Sexual Fantasies

Eroticism has been viewed as the "dirty," "kinky," or "exciting but bad" part of sex. Among comedians and in X-rated movies, the message is that erotic sex is the only type of sex that matters. Our mantra of intimacy, pleasuring, and eroticism with integrated couple sexuality is discarded and even mocked. "Real sex" is erotic sex focused on genitals, intercourse, and orgasm; the rest is fluff. Even more powerful (and destructive) meanings of eroticism come from sex magazines, the Internet, porn videos, and erotic books. One theme is that the crazier and higher risk the situation, the more erotic. The second theme is the crazier the woman, the more erotic she is. If you accept this as a fantasy model that has no relevance to real-life couples and their couple sexual style, you would be okay. Otherwise, it is a very destructive message.

The healthy function of erotic fantasies is to serve as a bridge to desire and as a special erotic charge to facilitate arousal and orgasm. The danger comes when people take this fantasy view of eroticism seriously and try to translate it to real-life behavior. In the great majority of cases, these make better erotic fantasies than erotic behavior for real-life couples. In truth, sexual fantasy and erotic behavior belong to very different realms.

Contrary to movies and love songs, arousal is not always easy or automatic. When touch progresses from comfort to pleasure to eroticism, it is easier to facilitate receptivity and responsivity to erotic encounters. In other words, most of the time you don't jump into eroticism; it develops through the bridges of intimacy and pleasuring. "Sexual drag racing" is the term we use for the man who tries to go from "0 to 100" (orgasm) as fast as he can. Although occasional "quickies" and beginning an encounter in a highly erotic manner adds spice to your sexual relationship, if that's the prime focus, your sexual relationship will quickly burn out, leaving you demoralized and experiencing inhibited sexual desire.

Cognitive and Behavioral Continuums of Arousal

Think of arousal on a 10-point scale: 0 is neutral, 3 is feeling sensual and receptive, 5 signals beginning levels of arousal with vaginal lubrication and erection, 8 involves high levels of erotic flow, and 10 is being orgasmic. Eroticism refers to the 6 to 10 phase, enjoying your erotic flow to high levels of arousal and orgasm. Eroticism involves scenarios and techniques that focus on heightening arousal, combined with manual, oral, rubbing, vibrator, and intercourse stimulation. The key is being receptive and responsive to erotic scenarios and techniques.

What interferes with genital stimulation and erotic flow? The major factor is self-consciousness. Sex is not a spectator sport. The major erotic stimulus is an involved, responsive partner. Anticipatory anxiety, performance anxiety, and spectatoring subvert eroticism. A key is to set the stage so you and your partner are receptive and responsive to erotic scenarios and techniques. The challenge is to integrate intimacy and eroticism into your couple sexual style.

There is a complex relationship between subjective and objective arousal. You want to feel "turned on" as well as experiencing objective physiological arousal in terms of lubrication and erection. Typically, subjective arousal leads objective arousal by allowing you to anticipate a sexual encounter, be receptive to touch and pleasure, be responsive to genital stimulation, and allow yourself to enter into an erotic flow to orgasm.

The Three Styles of Arousal

There are three primary arousal styles. In order of frequency these are (1) partner interaction arousal, (2) self-entrancement arousal, and (3) role enactment arousal. By far the most common is partner interaction arousal. This is the arousal pattern shown on TV and in movies. It follows the famous Masters and Johnson pleasure guideline—"give to get." Each person's arousal plays off the other's. The major aphrodisiac is an aroused partner. The focus of arousal is interaction, whether mutual touching or taking turns. The partners are looking at each other, talking (whether romantic or erotic), and feeling a mutual turn-on. The touching techniques can be varied and unpredictable—whatever turns you and your partner on. Partner interaction arousal is both intimate and erotic. Some couples never use other arousal styles.

Self-entrancement arousal focuses on mental and physical relaxation, being receptive and responsive to touch and physical sensations. This arousal style works best when you take turns. The receiver is passive, eyes closed, relaxed, receiving stylized and consistent touch. The internal focus is on being relaxed, receptive to touch and taking in pleasurable sensations. Some couples begin with self-entrancement arousal and then transition to partner interaction arousal to build erotic flow. Self-entrancement arousal is commonly used in one-way sexual scenarios.

Role enactment arousal focuses on external stimuli to build eroticism. This is the fun and "out-there" style. Eroticism is the focus, downplaying intimacy and pleasuring. Examples include use of sexual toys such as a vibrator or a fur mitt, playing out a bondage and discipline scenario, use of R-rated or X-rated videos, playing out a fantasy scenario such as virgin–prostitute or one-night stand, and engaging in erotic dancing or striptease. The key is to build a strong erotic charge, not a gradual pleasure-oriented build-up. Because intimacy is underplayed and eroticism and external stimuli are so highly valued, some couples (especially women) do not find this arousal style personally inviting.

All three arousal styles can enhance eroticism. You can choose whether to utilize all three, focus on two (partner interaction and self-entrancement are most common), or use only one (usually partner interaction). Be aware that erotic scenarios and techniques are necessary for high arousal and orgasm. Intimacy and pleasuring are valuable but are not enough to generate and maintain erotic flow.

Erotic Fantasies

During partner sex, about 70% of men and 50% of women use erotic fantasies, at least on occasion. Many people use erotic fantasies on a regular basis. By their very nature, erotic fantasies are not socially acceptable. Almost no one fantasizes about having sex with their spouse in their bedroom using man-on-top intercourse. The most frequent erotic fantasies involve a different partner, forced or forcing sex, group or triadic sex, being observed or observing someone else being sexual, or sex with someone of the same gender. In other words, erotic fantasies emphasize people and scenarios that are totally outside the reality of your sex life. Does that mean what you really want is to play out your erotic fantasies? For the great majority of people, fantasies are in a totally different domain than real-life behavior. That's what makes the fantasy an erotic turn-on. For most couples, the result of playing out fantasies is disappointment. The erotic charge is much higher in the fantasy mode than in reality.

What is the healthy function of erotic fantasies? They serve as a bridge to sexual desire and as a means to enhance arousal and orgasm. Erotic fantasies help you be a more involved, aroused partner. Fantasy enhances the individual and couple eroticism process. It is something to welcome and enjoy, not to be afraid of or defensive about.

Are there situations where fantasies can be misused? Of course, but that's true of any aspect of sexuality. The most common problem is when the fantasy operates as a wall rather than a bridge. An example is a man with a fetish arousal pattern who uses the fetish fantasy to wall off (shut down and avoid) his partner because she interferes with the narrow controlling fetish. A different example is the woman burdened by guilt because she is afraid of and/or ashamed of her fantasies. Guilt and fear feed a compulsive sexual cycle to make these fantasies dominant and controlling. The answer is to accept your fantasies and allow them to be eclectic rather than narrow. Remember, fantasy and behavior are totally different realms.

A third possible problem is that your partner is worried about your fantasies, feeling rejected and believing that you really want the fantasy, not him or her. Enjoying erotic fantasy is not being disloyal; it is healthy and normal. We use the analogy of a famous movie star who said, "I know 100,000 men go to sleep each night fantasizing about having sex with me, but I can't have sex in my marriage." Real-life sex and real-life couples are totally different than movie sex and fantasy sex.

Of course, erotic fantasies and erotic materials can be misused and subvert couple sex. This is a special trap for males who fall into a sexual life of high eroticism, high shame, and secrecy—a powerful and destructive combination—over a variant arousal pattern, often on the Internet. Compulsive sex is not healthy sex. The key for healthy sexuality is to regard erotic fantasies as a bridge to intimate, interactive couple sex.

The Good, the Bad, and the Erotic

Erotic sex has a bad name in the marriage, conservative, religious, and even legal communities. The association is with "dirty, but exciting" sex as depicted in porn videos. The fear is that eroticism will cause one or both partners to act out and destabilize your relationship. People trust intimate sex, but not intimate, erotic sex. Can a sole focus on eroticism subvert or even destroy a relationship? Yes, it can. However, erotic sex between committed couples is different than high-risk sex, porn sex, or using sex to prove you're liberated. The challenge for individuals and couples is to integrate intimacy and eroticism so there is greater emotional and sexual satisfaction. At its essence eroticism is good, not bad. The key is to experience integrated eroticism so that it enhances the person's and couple's sexual satisfaction.

Warren and Leila Warren had been divorced for five years and Leila for nine years. Sex was not the major issue in their respective divorces, but as the marriage deteriorated, so did the sexual relationship. Warren especially felt wounded by his ex-wife's verbal barbs aimed at his sexual technique and confidence. For Leila, the immediate effect of her divorce was to cause inhibited sexual desire.

The dating game as a single-again adult is quite different than premarital dating. There is less optimism and more emphasis on proving yourself personally and sexually. Leila's sexual desire and response were temporarily restored, but she grew tired of the dating/sex scene. Warren's post-marriage experience had been difficult. He'd had three serious dating relationships. At the beginning he experienced performance anxiety, but with time and Viagra the sex improved. However, sex cannot save a fragile relationship. In all three situations, it was the women who ended the relationship; Warren experienced these as further rejections.

Leila and Warren approached their relationship very slowly. They were introduced 19 months previously through mutual friends who organized a playground-building beer and pizza activity. Warren was quite good at carpentry, and Leila was impressed by both his good skills and good humor. Leila was the custodial parent for her 13-year-old son. She wished her ex-spouse would help their son learn "masculine" skills instead of being the "fun father." Warren had no children but enjoyed his friends' children and doing the good deed of building the playground for neighborhood kids. In talking with Leila over beer and pizza, Warren suggested that her son play on a select community soccer team for which he was the assistant coach.

Over the ensuing weeks, Leila was aware of a growing attraction to Warren, and after a soccer game she invited him to her house for lunch. The attraction was mutual, but Warren was hesitant, both because of sexual performance anxiety and fear that if they had a failed relationship it would affect her son and the soccer team. This is a common dilemma for adult, non-married couples. However, rather than back off, Leila encouraged the relationship. She suggested they compartmentalize the soccer/coaching element from the romantic/sexual relationship. The system Leila had put in place with other men she had dated could work with Warren. She did not introduce the man to her son until they'd been dating at least six months, at which point they were likely to continue together. Leila and Warren would not let her son know of their relationship until they were sure they'd be a serious couple.

Since Leila and Warren had been able to discuss and reach an agreement about this sensitive emotional issue, it promoted their ability to discuss sensitive sexual issues. This was the first time Warren had talked about sex before having sex. In her nine years of dating, Leila was familiar with erection problems. As a married woman in her 20s, Leila believed that erection problems only occurred with men older than 60, but as a 38-year-old divorced woman Leila was aware that many men experienced erectile anxiety in their 30s and 40s. Normalizing this was very helpful for Warren. The most helpful move was Leila's proposal to take the lead in designing the sexual scenario.

Leila's suggestion was for Warren to relax, be open to pleasuring, and be more than a spectator. Leila's focus was on erotic scenarios and techniques, rather than intimacy and pleasuring. This was not to raise Warren's performance expectations but to focus him on enjoying visual stimulation and erotic touch. Leila's "sexual voice" was playful and unpredictable, and she enjoyed both role enactment and partner interaction arousal. Her favorite erotic scenario was Warren being passive while she played with him in a seductive manner —starting with oral stimulation, switching to rubbing against him, then holding him and starting and stopping manual stimulation. Leila liked dressing in a sexy bra that opened in the front, high-heeled shoes, and no underwear. It was Leila who decided when to transition to intercourse with her guiding intromission from the woman-on-top or side-rear entry position. Warren was responsive to this combination of playful and erotic stimulation and "piggy-backed" his arousal on Leila's. Warren was surprised that he quickly overcame his self-consciousness and spectatoring, and regained comfort and confidence with erections. Leila's eroticism was very inviting for him, and success breeds success.

His Eroticism, Her Eroticism, and Our Eroticism

Like bridges to sexual desire, different people have different erotic preferences. Traditionally, men prefer mutual stimulation, multiple stimulation, visual stimulation, focus on arousing their partner, and being orgasmic during intercourse. Female erotic preferences are more variable and individualistic. About three of four women prefer multiple stimulation, and two of three women prefer mutual stimulation. More women than men prefer self-entrancement arousal, and female orgasmic response is more variable and complex than male orgasm. She might be singly orgasmic, non-orgasmic, or multi-orgasmic. Orgasm might occur during the pleasuring/foreplay phase, during intercourse, or in the afterplay phase. For males, function and satisfaction are closely associated; he values predictable intercourse and orgasm at each encounter. Some women report high levels of pleasure and satisfaction with non-orgasmic experiences; less than 20% of women are orgasmic during every encounter.

Both men and women say partner interaction arousal is the most common pattern. Although there are large individual and couple differences, in general men are more likely to prefer role enactment arousal (the major exception being that women are more likely to use vibrator stimulation) and women prefer self-entrancement arousal. Women are more likely to prefer a sequence of receiving non-genital and then genital stimulation, while men value receiving genital stimulation (but only when they are already aroused). Women are more likely to request multiple stimulation during intercourse—especially manual clitoral stimulation.

One of the most helpful psychosexual skill exercises is to initiate and play out your favorite sexual scenario. Each person gets a turn. One partner initiates in his/her favorite manner (bridges to desire), sets up their favorite pleasuring scenario, decides when and how to transition from pleasuring to eroticism, introduces their favorite erotic scenario and technique, decides when to transition to intercourse and guides intromission, chooses whether to use multiple stimulation during intercourse, and plays out their favorite afterplay scenario. When it's the other partner's turn to initiate his or her favorite sexual scenario, it is clear they are different sexual people with different sexual preferences. Acceptance of erotic differences enhances your couple sexual style and sexual satisfaction.

Does your partner have to enjoy your erotic scenario? Ideally, he or she would find it highly inviting and erotic. If this occurs, you are a very lucky couple. More commonly, the partner accepts your erotic scenario and enjoys it because you enjoy it. The partner is pleased with the outcome because your erotic turn-on feeds his/her sexual arousal. At other times, the partner's response might be neutral or even mildly negative toward your scenario, but he or she "goes along for the ride" and is fine about being a good sexual friend. This is perfectly acceptable and encourages you to enjoy your erotic scenario.

A potential problem is that too many couples develop hurt feelings and get into a power struggle. One partner feels sexually rejected or not loved if the other partner isn't really turned on. Be cognizant that you are not clones of each other. What is erotic for you may not be erotic for your partner. That's normal. It's not intended as a rejection, and there's no need to react to it as a rejection. Our suggestion is to enjoy your erotic scenario, and reinforce your partner for being a good sexual friend.

Now the really hard issue: What if your partner finds your erotic scenario a turn-off and is not open to engaging in it? A prime guideline is that sex is about sharing pleasure, not a power struggle. Using intimate coercion poisons couple sexuality. Accept the disappointing reality that your erotic scenario will not work in this relationship. Your partner's emotional needs are more important than your erotic needs. You can identify and play out a different erotic scenario. You can find common ground sexually without negating your partner's emotional and sexual comfort.

A good example involves a man who was highly aroused by a role enactment arousal scenario in which his partner dressed in an erotic outfit with her vulva exposed and her legs spread while he put breast clamps on her and did oral sex to orgasm as she begged him to stop. In fact, she enjoyed receiving oral sex, loved shopping at Victoria's Secret, and was open to role enactment arousal and erotic talk. However, she found his scenario "over the top"; it was too rigid and demeaning. She offered an alternative scenario, but he wisely said no; "watering it down" would cause the loss of erotic charge. Instead, he suggested a different erotic scenario focused on combining role enactment and partner interaction arousal.

Exercise: Creating Erotic Couple Scenarios

You do not have to prove anything to yourself, your partner, or anyone else during this exercise. Focus on exploring erotic turn-ons, both yours and your partner's. One of the most fascinating aspects of sexuality is accepting the wide diversity of what people find erotic.

Request and share erotic scenarios and techniques that heighten your desire and arousal. He can take the first initiative. Think of erotic scenarios and techniques as a smorgasbord: slow, mutual, passionate kissing followed by rapid, intense intercourse; role enactment arousal using an R- or X-rated video to enhance eroticism; touching and playing in the shower and then having oral sex to orgasm when you are clean and fresh; reading erotic fantasies to your partner and not touching until she is highly desirous and receptive; quick, intense intercourse where you really enjoy coming and then use your hand to give her as many orgasms as she wants; intercourse in the rear-entry position with deep thrusting or with her sitting and you kneeling so you can give and receive manual stimulation; mixing mutual manual and oral stimulation until both of you are highly aroused and then switching to intercourse with the woman on top guiding intromission; self-entrancement arousal where you are passive, relaxed, accept her stimulation, and then transition to the rear-entry position using simultaneous manual clitoral stimulation; multiple stimulation during intercourse in which she strokes your testicles and you engage in manual clitoral stimulation and kiss her breasts; having your partner orally stimulate you when you are standing and she is kneeling, which some men prefer to carry to orgasm while others want to transition to intercourse; he orally stimulating her and she choosing whether to proceed to orgasm or switch to intercourse at high levels of erotic flow. We encourage you to choose a favorite scenario and really enjoy playing it out. When it is the woman's turn we encourage her to play out her favorite erotic scenario; this should reflect her sexual voice, which may be similar to his or quite different.

Each person should initiate/play out his or her erotic scenario(s). Remember, however, that this is not a competition. Share arousing and erotic feelings. Be free to take emotional and sexual risks with each other. If either partner feels that something being proposed is physically or psychologically negative, the other partner has the power to use a veto, which will be honored. Eroticism is about being creative, emotionally and sexually taking risks; it should encourage unpredictability, not intimidation.

Whether creating erotic scenarios individually or mutually, be open to each other's feelings and requests. Do not put up artificial barriers between erotic sex play and intercourse. Experiment with taking turns and mutual stimulation; focus on mixing self-entrancement arousal, partner interaction arousal, and role enactment arousal; play with single and multiple stimulation; mix non-verbal and verbal sexual communication; view intercourse as a natural extension of the pleasuring/eroticism process and transition to intercourse at high levels of arousal. Enjoy creative, flowing, erotic sexuality. Creativity does not end with orgasm. Experiment with afterplay scenarios and techniques that put a satisfying closure to your erotic experience.

Intimacy and Eroticism

The challenge for all couples, married or unmarried, is to integrate intimacy and eroticism into their relationship. Erotic scenarios and techniques build anticipatory desire, pleasure, and arousal, and result in erotic flow to orgasm. Intimacy—feeling close, connected, safe—and eroticism—taking risks, savoring unpredictability, functioning at high levels of emotion and arousal—are complementary expressions of sexual desire and can be integrated to enhance couple sexual satisfaction.

Closing Thoughts

Eroticism has traditionally been viewed as "dirty" or "kinky," a side component of couple sexuality and more the man's domain. We hope this chapter has helped you understand and accept eroticism as a positive, integrated part of your couple sexual style. Eroticism is an integral component of the intimacy/pleasuring/eroticism cycle of healthy, satisfying sexuality. It is as much the woman's domain as the man's. Eroticism is the special part of sexuality that allows a sense of both high subjective arousal and high physiological arousal. Eroticism provides a special charge to your couple sexual style.

CHAPTER **8**

Optimizing Sexual Intercourse

For most couples in most cultures "sex equals intercourse." People believe that intercourse is natural and instinctive. Yet 70% of intercourse among American couples is in the man-on-top position done in a routine, mechanical manner. Typically, the man initiates intercourse when he feels the woman is ready and guides intromission (putting his penis in her vagina). The traditional goal is simultaneous orgasm during intercourse, which can be intimidating rather than an empowering goal and which is seldom achieved.

It's hoped that you find that intercourse sex is comfortable and functional, but if that's the only way to proceed it will become boring at best and a turn-off at worst. Men and women have traditionally attached different meanings to intercourse. For the man, intercourse is the pass–fail performance test. He predictably has one orgasm that occurs during intercourse. Intimacy and foreplay is for her, intercourse for him. The man on top is the "natural" position because he can be in charge and his penis won't slip out of her vagina. For most women, intercourse is an integral part of the lovemaking process—the main course but not the only course.

Physically and emotionally, intercourse involves the greatest sense of connection. In terms of orgasm, only about one in four women have the same orgasm pattern as men—a single orgasm during intercourse with no additional stimulation. Two of three women are able to be orgasmic with intercourse using multiple stimulation, especially clitoral stimulation. However, about one in three women are never or almost never orgasmic during intercourse. This is normal, not dysfunctional, and doesn't mean the woman and the couple don't value their intercourse experience. Less than 20% of women are orgasmic at each sexual encounter. But this statistic does not negate the value of the sexual experience. It is an example of variable, flexible female and couple sexuality.

Throughout this book we emphasize sexual communication and options and encourage you to develop a variable, flexible couple sexual style that emphasizes pleasure and satisfaction. So how can we help you enjoy your intercourse experience in this context?

The single most important concept is to view intercourse as a natural extension of the pleasuring/eroticism process, not a performance test. This involves two crucially important techniques. The first is to transition to intercourse at high levels of arousal—at 7 or 8 rather than at 4 or 5 on a 10-point scale. The second technique is to value sexual experimentation, especially multiple stimulation during intercourse. The typical lovemaking scenario lasts between 15–45 minutes, of which intercourse itself involves 2–7 minutes. Contrary to media myths and porn videos, very few couples have intercourse that extends over 12–15 minutes. Of course, you can enjoy a one-minute quickie as well as an extended lovemaking scenario.

Both men and women place high value on intercourse, both physically and emotionally. Intercourse is a special pleasuring experience with an emphasis on mutuality. There is a recognition that intercourse can serve different needs at different times. Couples rely on intercourse to (1) share pleasure, (2) reduce tension, (3) deepen intimacy, (4) reinforce self-esteem and desirability, and (5) meet the traditional biological function of achieving pregnancy. It is normal and healthy to have different needs over time and even day to day. It is also normal that each partner might engage in intercourse for a different reason(s). On occasion, intercourse meets special needs—e.g., reconnecting after weeks apart or after an argument, being playful and creative, as part of a healing process after the funeral of a parent, celebrating a promotion, using it as a way to relax and facilitate sleep, rebuilding self-esteem after a failed business project, or celebrate the wedding of your child.

Intercourse Positions

For some couples the only type of intercourse is man on top using short, rapid thrusting. Unfortunately, many of these couples also deal with premature ejaculation. Each intercourse position has its strengths as well as potential vulnerabilities (which is also true of types of thrusting and types of stimulation during intercourse).

Why is man on top the most popular intercourse position? It's the easiest position for a man to guide intromission, control thrusting, and maintain penile-vaginal connection. People feel this is the biologically "natural" position (although some cultures don't even know of it). This is the best position to achieve pregnancy. Some women report they feel safest and most connected with man-on-top intercourse. The biggest problem is that it reinforces rigid male–female sex roles. Also, this is a harder position in which to utilize multiple stimulation (especially clitoral stimulation). Then there's the premature ejaculation problem, female passivity, and the reality that the out-of-shape male finds it physically stressful. This position allows good eye contact but not visual stimuli from other body parts. Perhaps the greatest vulnerability is that sex becomes routine and mechanical.

The second most common intercourse position is woman on top. An oft-stated advantage is to give the woman more symbolic and actual physical control, especially of thrusting movements and rhythm. This is a good position for multiple stimulation of the clitoris, breasts, buttocks, and anal area. It provides the man with visual stimulation of her body and arousal. He still could control the thrusting, especially if he uses her buttocks for leverage. There are potential vulnerabilities with woman-on-top intercourse. Chief among these are that the woman is self-conscious and feels exposed and observed, and the man feels uncomfortable in the passive role and experiences this as anti-erotic. Many men (and women) react with anxiety if the penis slips out of the vagina. Some women feel it is difficult to meet the man's sexual expectations of taking the lead and being highly erotic.

With all intercourse positions there are a number of variations, and nowhere is this truer than in the side-by-side position. A major advantage is that this is an excellent position for multiple stimulation and switching who controls intercourse thrusting. In the 1970s a variation of the side-by-side position, lateral coital, was touted as the ideal intercourse position and was predicted to sweep across the world. Obviously, this did not occur even though scientifically lateral coital intercourse has considerable strengths—much body contact, visual connection, ablility to switch active/passive roles and take a break to talk, feeling comfortable and connected. Unfortunately, it proved too acrobatic for most couples. Also, if the penis slipped out of the vagina it was extremely difficult to reinsert from the lateral coital position, so the couple had to start over, which proved too awkward and self-conscious for most couples.

In regular side-by-side variations a strong advantage is that you can experiment with circular thrusting, and there is a great sense of mutuality. It is a wonderful position for multiple stimulation and is not physically taxing for either partner. This can be a playful intercourse position. Rear-entry side position is especially good during late-stage pregnancy. Vulnerabilities include that it requires being open to shifting positions so everything "fits," it requires cooperation and mutuality, and the penis can slip out. It requires willingness to be flexible if something doesn't work and requires more verbal and non-verbal communication that other positions. The couple needs to be cooperative and flexible to really enjoy side-by-side intercourse.

The rear-entry ("doggie") intercourse position can be one of the most erotic and provides for deeper penile penetration. It also allows for manual clitoral stimulation with his hand or hers. It gives the feeling of an experimental, edgy, erotic scenario and thus can "spice up" your couple sexuality. Couples feel permission to let go sexually and go with erotic feelings. Many men find that giving buttock stimulation during intercourse is a turn-on. The absence of eye contact allows each partner to focus on erotic fantasies. In terms of potential disadvantages, this has been viewed as an "animalistic" position and somehow degrading to the woman. Many people complain of missing the intimacy that comes from eye contact and kissing. Some people associate this vaginal intercourse position with anal intercourse and worry about a hidden sexual agenda.

In addition to these four classic positions, there are a multitude of others, as well as combinations and variations. The advantage of experimenting with intercourse positions is to enhance variability and eroticism, which can include switching intercourse positions during an encounter. For example, many couples begin with woman-on-top, which is more erotic for her, then switch to man-on-top or rear-entry, which is more erotic for him. Couples will also vary positions. At times they are prone, at other times she will wrap her legs around his body, and at still other times extend her legs to his shoulders. The goal is to increase involvement and creativity rather than proceed with a predictable routine.

Rather than studying the *Kamasutra* and trying to develop 50 different intercourse positions, most couples experiment with one to three additional positions. An example is the sitting/kneeling intercourse position, originally developed for late-stage pregnancy because it puts minimal pressure on the woman's stomach. Many couples continue to use this position, at least on occasion, since it provides different sensations and types of stimulation. Typically, the woman uses a pillow behind her back for support and the man kneels on a pillow, both to raise his body so his penis is at the same height as her vulva as well as to offer support for his knees. This position allows both partners' hands to be free for multiple stimulation. In addition, they can maintain eye contact and kiss; they can alternate who controls intercourse thrusting and utilize circular thrusting; they can take a break and talk while he stays inside her; and it is an excellent position for clitoral stimulation with his hand or hers.

Movement and Stimulation During Intercourse

Every couple develops its unique style of intercourse positions, movements, and stimulation. There is no one "right" way to have intercourse, no matter what is written in popular media. Some couples prefer very predictable intercourse while others like to experiment with two or three variations;

other couples use every variation possible and make up some of their own. What is comfortable and enjoyable for your couple sexual style?

You and your partner probably have different movement preferences. That's normal, so don't allow these differences to become a "right–wrong" power struggle. Rather, make use of various techniques on different occasions— circular thrusting; in–out stroking; slow, deep thrusting; rapid in–out thrusting; and up–down thrusting. Sometimes the woman can control the thrusting type and rhythm, and at other times he can. The guideline is not to do something that is uncomfortable or a turn-off for either partner. Each person has a right to veto what he/she finds aversive and to trust that the partner will respect his/her veto. Even more important, each partner can be emotionally generous in accepting the other's preferences and turn-ons.

This guideline is even more important in terms of multiple stimulation during intercourse. Approximately three of four people prefer multiple stimulation during the pleasuring/eroticism phase. Why stop multiple stimulation when his penis is inside her vagina? The majority of couples find that multiple stimulation during intercourse increases involvement and arousal. This is especially true of males with erectile anxiety and ejaculatory inhibition, as well as women who experience arousal or orgasm problems.

The most common multiple stimulation technique is use of erotic fantasies as a bridge to arousal and orgasm. Many individuals (women as well as men) use erotic fantasies during couple sex. Most couples find that fantasies work better as fantasies rather than verbalizing them or acting them out. The second most common technique is utilizing additional touch— using his or her fingers for clitoral stimulation, giving or receiving breast or anal stimulation, stimulating testicles manually, indulging in romantic or erotic talk. Couples can switch intercourse positions or withdraw from intercourse and use oral/manual/rubbing stimulation to high arousal and then transition back to intercourse. Multiple stimulation is particularly valuable with partner interaction arousal. Each person's arousal plays off the other person's—the "give to get" guideline applied to intercourse.

Jeremy and Jocelyn Jeremy and Jocelyn had very different experiences and attached different meanings to intercourse. Jeremy saw himself as enjoying the entire sexual encounter, but intercourse was definitely his favorite part. Throughout his 20s, 30s, and 40s, each sexual experience culminated with intercourse. Although he enjoyed manual and oral stimulation, he regarded intercourse as "real sex." Jeremy found intercourse easy and predictable. Jocelyn certainly valued intercourse as an integral part of their sexual experience, but she felt that sex was much more than intercourse. In fact, a source of dissatisfaction is that Jeremy would switch to intercourse just when Jocelyn was really getting into the erotic flow, which was disrupted by the abrupt switch and cessation of multiple stimulation. Although at times Jocelyn really enjoyed intercourse, she very much enjoyed manual and oral stimulation. She told her girlfriends that intercourse was four stars, but cunnilingus was five stars.

Couple sexuality started changing when they were in their early 50s. Jeremy began to be self-conscious about his erections. Arousal and erection became slower, less easy, and less predictable. Jeremy initiated intercourse the minute his erection was firm enough. Jocelyn felt their lovemaking was less about mutuality and more about Jeremy's penis. He was so afraid of an intercourse failure that he was much less attentive to her touch. Instead he was a distracted spectator focused on the state of his penis. Sex was no longer about intimacy, pleasuring, and eroticism that flowed to intercourse. Instead, sex was about Jeremy's penis and whether it would succeed or fail at intercourse.

Without speaking to Jocelyn about it, Jeremy purchased Viagra through the Internet. Jocelyn had two concerns. He was taking a prescription medication without consulting a physician. Just as important, instead of turning to Jocelyn to rebuild comfort with erections and intercourse, he turned to a medication and shut her out. Rather than intercourse bringing them together, it was putting a wedge between them. Jocelyn saw Jeremy as becoming obsessed with intercourse as a pass–fail test. Jeremy felt that Jocelyn did not understand the pressure he felt as a man not to fail at intercourse.

Instead of being on the same intimate team, Jeremy and Jocelyn felt misunderstood and alienated, especially regarding the meaning of intercourse. Rather than treating this with benign neglect and allowing the sex problem to become more chronic and severe, they made a wise decision to consult a marriage therapist with a sub-specialty in sexual dysfunction. The clinician scheduled the first session as a couple session, then set up individual sessions to delve into each partner's psychological, relational, and sexual history and feelings about the erection problem and intercourse.

At the couple feedback session, the clinician said in a supportive, empathic way that Jeremy and Jocelyn needed to develop a new couple sexual style that fit the reality of being in their 50s instead of trying to recapture the sexuality of their 20s. Specifically, Jeremy needed to turn toward Jocelyn both emotionally and physically. They needed to jointly figure out how to integrate Viagra into their couple sexual style. Most important, they needed to adopt the Good Enough Sex Model for intercourse, in which they could positively anticipate a sexual encounter flowing to intercourse about 85% of the time and when it didn't accept a transition to an erotic, non-intercourse scenario or a cuddly, sensual scenario. The clinician also suggested that Jocelyn initiate the transition to intercourse and guide intromission so that Jeremy could focus on the pleasuring/erotic flow. In addition, Jeremy needed to be open to sharing orgasm (hers and his) with manual, oral, or rubbing stimulation rather than insisting that the only satisfying sex must involve orgasm during intercourse.

Jocelyn was very enthusiastic about this new approach to intercourse and couple sex. She was especially intrigued with the idea that if they could learn this new couple approach to intercourse it would inoculate them against sexual problems so they could enjoy a satisfying sexuality in their 60s, 70s, and 80s. Jeremy agreed to try these new strategies and techniques, but was worried they could make sex worse.

Nothing succeeds like success. Jocelyn's obvious enjoyment of their new couple sexual style eventually won Jeremy over. An involved, aroused partner is the major aphrodisiac. Jeremy learned to "piggy-back" his arousal on hers. In fact, Jocelyn joked that they did better than most couples since 90% of their encounters flowed to intercourse. Jeremy phased out his Viagra use (although he would occasionally take Viagra to boost confidence or during stressful times). Intercourse became a positive, integral part of their couple sexual style, but it was now a mutual, vital, and flexible style of intercourse.

Can You Have Good Sex Without Intercourse?

The answer to the question is definitely yes. Couples can enjoy a vital and satisfying sexuality without intercourse. But why choose to do that? Typically couples avoid intercourse because of negative motivations. For males it is fear of failure; for females it is fear of pain or feeling she is not good at intercourse. Such negative motivation almost never promotes healthy sexual behavior.

Intercourse is a choice, not a mandate. We encourage you to enjoy a variable, flexible couple sexuality that includes, but is not controlled by, intercourse. Once they break free from the pass–fail perfect intercourse performance criterion, most couples choose to invite intercourse as a natural continuation of the pleasuring/eroticism process while remaining open to erotic, non-intercourse, and/or sensual scenarios.

Exercise: Integrating Intercourse Into Your Couple Style of Intimacy, Pleasuring, and Eroticism

This can be one of the most meaningful exercises for your couple sexual style. The exercise is divided into three phases: (1) Write down the five scenarios and techniques you most value about intercourse and one to three aspects of intercourse you want to veto, with your partner accepting your veto without hassling; (2) discuss intercourse scenarios—transition from eroticism to intercourse, intercourse positions, intercourse movements, and multiple stimulation during intercourse. Be specific about what contributes to your sexual satisfaction and what subverts your satisfaction; (3) play out at least one intercourse scenario designed by her and one designed by him. Ideally each partner plays out two of his/her favorite intercourse scenarios.

In all three phases we urge you to be as personal, specific, and concrete as possible. Your intercourse preferences and feelings are very important to your couple sexual style and satisfaction.

Closing Thoughts

Intercourse is a very special couple experience, both physically and emotionally, that integrates intimacy and eroticism. We believe intercourse is the most integrative of all sexual experiences and has the potential to give your sexual relationship a very special meaning.

We hope you have heeded the warning in this chapter about confrontation and negativity. Don't allow couple sexuality to be subverted by the traditional male emphasis on perfect intercourse performance. Instead be guided by this chapter's core positive message: that intercourse is best integrated into your sexual style as a natural continuation of the pleasuring/eroticism process. Identify and play out your preferred intercourse scenarios—positions, movements, multiple stimulation. If sex doesn't flow into intercourse, you can enjoy sensual sex or erotic, non-intercourse sex. Value intercourse as a special component of your couple sexual style of intimacy, pleasuring, and eroticism.

CHAPTER **9**

Savoring Orgasm and Afterplay

Is orgasm the most important part of sex? In the classic sex book of your grandparents, generation, *Ideal Marriage*, the goal for sexual satisfaction was simultaneous orgasm during intercourse. The performance myth of the ultimate pleasure of simultaneous orgasm served to oppress many, many couples. Old myths die hard. When it comes to orgasm, old myths are joined by a multitude of new myths. These myths state with certain authority the primacy of G-spot orgasms, multiple orgasms, one-hour extended orgasms, multi-orgasmic couples, or the man withholding orgasm so once a month he can experience an earth-shattering orgasm.

Like all sex therapy professionals, we are very pro-orgasm. Orgasm (climax) is the natural continuation of the desire, comfort, pleasure, arousal, erotic flow process. Orgasm is the natural result of sexual responsiveness, not a pass–fail test of your or your partner's sexual worth. Orgasm is an integral component of sexual satisfaction. However, it certainly is not the only, and in most cases, not even the most important, component in satisfaction. Like other aspects of sexuality, orgasm involves a paradox. In healthy couple sexuality, orgasm, among other things, plays a positive, integral role in achieving satisfaction. Paradoxically, orgasmic dysfunction or conflicts about orgasmic response can play an inordinately powerful negative role in couple dissatisfaction.

A key factor in healthy couple sexuality is understanding (both physically and psychologically) the similarities and differences in male and female orgasmic response. As we say throughout this book, couples do best when they accept that there are more similarities than differences between men and women in serious relationships. This is hard for many people to understand when it comes to the topic of orgasm because as adolescents and young adults sexual socialization and orgasmic experiences were so different. The great majority of men experience orgasm between 10 and 16 with masturbation or nocturnal emissions. In partner sex, the major male concern is the problem of premature (rapid) ejaculation. The first orgasmic experience is much more variable for adolescent and young adult women. Masturbation is the most reliable means to learn to be orgasmic, but it is less common among female adolescents. For many young women, orgasm first occurs during partner manual, oral, or rubbing stimulation. For both men and women, it is quite unusual for first orgasm to occur during intercourse. Typically, both men and women find orgasm enjoyable, but often it is mixed with feelings of embarrassment, self-consciousness, and guilt.

Perhaps the best way to state differences in orgasmic response for adult couples is that male orgasm is more predictable and stereotypic: He has one orgasm during intercourse. Although we have emphasized the common preference for regularity and predictability (a single orgasm during intercourse each time), that may or may not be true for the woman.

Female orgasmic response is more flexible and variable. She might have a single orgasm, multiple orgasms, or be non-orgasmic at that encounter. Orgasm can occur with manual, oral, rubbing, or vibrator stimulation before or after intercourse or she might be orgasmic during intercourse. In fact, only one in four women has the orgasmic response pattern of men: a single orgasm during intercourse with no additional stimulation. Two of three women are able to be orgasmic during intercourse.

Contrary to the cultural myth of the importance of length of intercourse, the truth is that for most women the key is multiple stimulation during intercourse, especially manual clitoral stimulation, and use of erotic fantasies as an orgasm trigger. Approximately one in five women has a multi-orgasmic response pattern, usually with manual or oral simulation. Few women—less than 20%—are orgasmic 100% of the time during partner sex. Most women find that a sexual encounter can be satisfying even when they are not orgasmic (this is traditionally not true for men). The most common scenario is that the woman is orgasmic in the pleasuring/foreplay phase and the man during intercourse, although many women enjoy a more variable orgasmic pattern (sometimes during intercourse and other times in the afterplay phase), and some men really enjoy receiving manual and/or oral sex to orgasm.

What does this information mean for your couple sexual style? Is male orgasmic response better than female orgasmic response, or vice versa? Our suggestion is to emphasize desire, pleasure, and satisfaction as a shared focus, and to accept differences and preferences in orgasmic response as a normal variation. Male orgasmic response is easier and more predictable. Female orgasmic response is not better or worse, just more variable and flexible. Her preferred orgasmic pattern is part of her sexual voice. The most common patterns are being orgasmic with manual stimulation during the pleasuring phase, being orgasmic using multiple stimulation during intercourse, a multi-orgasmic response during cunnilingus, a single orgasmic response during intercourse, or being orgasmic using manual or rubbing stimulation during afterplay. Other women have a different orgasmic response pattern: They use vibrator stimulation either during intercourse or afterplay, are orgasmic before and during intercourse, prefer taking turns and are orgasmic with self-entrancement arousal, or enjoy self-stimulation to orgasm while the partner holds and kisses them. The core concept is to honor diversity and for the woman (and the man) to enjoy her arousal/orgasm pattern(s).

Orgasmic Dysfunction

Is there genuine dysfunction in the area of orgasm? Yes. The most common male problem is premature ejaculation (PE). Most men begin their sex lives with PE, and about three in ten men worry at some point about premature ejaculation, which interferes with sexual satisfaction. More than 60% of young adults experience PE, and 25–30% of adults consistently experience PE. The common Internet and sex book advice is to reduce arousal (wear two condoms, think anti-erotic thoughts such as how much money you owe, masturbate before couple sex, use a penile desensitizing cream). This is always bad advice. You want to increase awareness and comfort, not decrease arousal. These tactics are more likely to result in more severe problems such as erectile dysfunction and inhibited sexual desire than they are to promote ejaculatory control. A healthy guideline for men (and women) is to "build comfort and awareness; never reduce arousal."

Learning ejaculatory control is a couple task with an emphasis on enhancing sexual satisfaction. It takes most couples three to six months to integrate ejaculatory control into intercourse and their couple sexual style. The man needs to learn to identify the point of ejaculatory inevitability and commit to learning self-entrancement arousal techniques (especially relaxing the pelvic muscles), and perhaps with a low dosage of anti-depressants. The couple should engage in woman-on-top intercourse, try circular thrusting, and slow down the lovemaking process.

Practical ejaculatory control skills can be learned both through masturbation and manual and oral stimulation. The woman can be an active ally in learning ejaculatory control. The couple works as an intimate team to share relaxation and pleasurable activities; experiment with intercourse positions (especially woman on top) and intercourse thrusting (particularly circular thrusting); and use the stop–start technique and the intercourse acclimation technique.

The second most frequent male orgasmic dysfunction is ejaculatory inhibition (EI). This is the hidden, ignored male sexual dysfunction. Approximately 1–2% of young males experience EI, specifically during intercourse. They are mistakenly viewed as "studs" by envious peers who suffer with PE. In truth, EI interferes with both male and couple sexual satisfaction.

The more common pattern is intermittent EI, which afects as many as 15% of men over 50. Men with EI want to be orgasmic but don't feel subjectively aroused or are unable to get into an erotic flow. EI is often misdiagnosed as erectile dysfunction because the man loses his erection during intercourse. This happens because he is frustrated that he's not able to "come" (reach orgasm), and he runs out of energy and loses his erection. EI (like other sexual problems) is best addressed as a couple. The key is to identify and confront the sexual inhibitions and for the man to regard the woman as his intimate, erotic friend, rather than someone to perform for. The key techniques are to transition to intercourse at high levels of subjective arousal, use multiple stimulation during intercourse, and make use of "orgasm triggers" to facilitate erotic flow to orgasm. Some men enjoy varying their orgasmic pattern to receive one-way stimulation focused on self-entrancement arousal and are orgasmic with manual or oral stimulation, at least on occasion.

Female orgasmic dysfunction is common, often based on lack of understanding of the woman's body and her sexual response. Again, the norm for female orgasmic response is that orgasm occurs in 65–85% of sexual encounters. Few women are orgasmic 100% of the time (although if that is her arousal/orgasmic pattern she and her partner can enjoy it). The most common sexual complaint (especially from males) is that the woman is not orgasmic during intercourse. In truth, this is a normal variation: One in three women is seldom or never orgasmic during intercourse.

The most common female orgasmic dysfunction involves women who had previously been orgasmic during partner sex but no longer are (secondary non-orgasmic response). The usual cause is that she has lost comfort and confidence in her desire/arousal/orgasm pattern. This could be a result of performance anxiety and unrealistic expectations, or partner pressure. More common is that the woman feels disappointed in herself, her partner, the relationship, or sex. Her desire and positive anticipation are inhibited/subverted. The reason she's no longer orgasmic is that she's not feeling aroused. Think of sexual arousal on a 10-point scale—with 0 as neutral, 3 as sensual, 5 as beginning arousal, 8 as into erotic flow, and 10 as orgasmic. If the woman's subjective arousal is less than 5, she or her partner is trying to force orgasm at low levels of arousal. She is fighting against her body rather than enjoying pleasure that leads to arousal, erotic flow, and naturally culminates in orgasm.

Other common problems include the power struggle whereby the woman's partner wants her to be orgasmic in a certain manner (during intercourse), or to be more expressive or intense during orgasm (have multiple orgasms, scream out, tell him what a great lover he is or how his penis feels inside her). The woman can become so self-conscious about not responding fast or powerfully enough that she becomes trapped in a self-conscious performance cycle.

Treatment strategies and techniques emphasize the one–two combination of the woman being responsible for her orgasm, and the couple working together as an intimate team to develop a comfortable, functional arousal and orgasm style. This involves confronting the inhibitions and turn-offs that subvert orgasm. Even more important is identifying the touch patterns and erotic scenarios that promote arousal, erotic flow, and orgasm. A generation ago, the issue of female orgasm was controlled by ignorance and silence. Since the advent of female orgasm books, female sexuality groups, focus on self-exploration and self-stimulation, use of vibrators, and increasing manual and oral stimulation, the number of women who have never been orgasmic has dramatically decreased.

Unfortunately, the number of women reporting secondary inhibited sexual desire and secondary non-orgasmic response has also dramatically increased. Typical "poisons" that subvert the desire/arousal/erotic flow/orgasm process include unrealistic performance demands (must have an orgasm each time, achieve a "G-spot" orgasm, be multi-orgasmic, have orgasm during intercourse without additional stimulation); anger or disappointment with the partner or relationship; a mechanistic sexual routine; and over-focus on intercourse sex.

Treatment strategies and techniques focus on the woman developing her "sexual voice" and the man acting as her intimate, erotic friend. Specifically, this means discovering if mutual stimulation or taking turns is more arousing; whether she prefers multiple or single stimulation; whether her preferred orgasmic pattern is with manual, oral intercourse, rubbing, or vibrator stimulation; whether orgasm occurs during the pleasuring, intercourse, or afterplay phase; whether erotic fantasies serve as a bridge to high arousal and orgasm; and whether her partner's orgasmic response is a cue for hers.

Clare and Darius Thirty-four-year-old Clare feels that she has finally developed her integrated sexual voice, which includes being orgasmic in more than 75% of sexual encounters with her husband of five years, Darius. Clare remembers as a 21-year-old college senior attending an intensive weekend female sexuality workshop focused on self-stimulation and using vibrators as well as "sexual toys" to enhance orgasmic response. Clare was orgasmic in more than 90% of masturbatory experiences, but found orgasm during couple sex more elusive and frustrating. She had boyfriends who would "do her" in ways that made her feel like a self-conscious performance machine, men who would apologize for their premature ejaculation and beg to manually stimulate her to orgasm, men who emphasized rough sex as the key to orgasm, and partners who tried to sequence their movements so there was simultaneous orgasm during intercourse.

Although she missed the excitement and unpredictability of dating and the sexual roller-coaster of a new romantic, passionate sex relationship, Clare felt more loving, safer, and more accepted in marital sex with Darius. This base of safety and sexual self-acceptance allowed Clare to develop her sexual voice and arousal/orgasm pattern. Clare enjoyed sexual variability and flexibility and teased Darius about settling for the "same old orgasm" during intercourse. Clare was most reliably orgasmic when receiving manual stimulation, and very much enjoyed touching and arousing Darius at the same time. Clare was usually singly orgasmic, but at times she would have additional orgasms either with continued manual stimulation or switching to intercourse at high levels of arousal. Interestingly, Darius enjoyed Clare's multi-orgasmic response (especially during intercourse) more than she did. Clare knew women who really enjoyed multi-orgasmic response, but Clare did not find it special or satisfying.

Clare means it when she says she likes variability. For example, in the sitting/kneeling intercourse position (which she learned during her pregnancy), Clare was often orgasmic using multiple stimulation during intercourse. Other times, especially if she had had one or two glasses of wine, Clare was open to giving and receiving oral stimulation and could be multi-orgasmic. At times, Clare would surprise Darius and say how warm and satisfied she felt about a sexual encounter in which she was non-orgasmic (there were other non-orgasmic experiences that felt neutral or frustrating).

Clare particularly valued the afterplay/afterglow lovemaking phase. It had taken a couple of years of lobbying Darius, but he, too, came to value their afterplay scenarios. Darius preferred to cuddle and engage in romantic talk, but Clare enjoyed a more active, involved afterplay scenario, especially if it was not late at night. Clare enjoyed showering together and being playful in the shower. Her other favorite afterplay scenario was when Darius made a cup of tea and they read about activities and events to plan for in the coming weeks.

Afterplay

Afterplay is the most neglected phase of the lovemaking process, yet it very much affects couple sexual satisfaction. This is a missed opportunity because spending physical and emotional time after a sexual experience presents an ideal milieu for bonding—whether through cuddling, playing, or talking. Afterplay is the time to focus on feelings of satisfaction, an acknowledgment of the intimacy and eroticism of your couple sexuality. Afterplay can be particularly important if the encounter was mediocre, dissatisfying, or dysfunctional. Afterplay is a positive way to end the encounter so the couple doesn't fall into the "apologize–blame" or "attack–counterattack" trap. Instead they end the experience in a warm, cuddly manner with the commitment to be sexual in the next one to three days when they are more awake, alert, and receptive. Spending physical and emotional time after a sexual encounter is an ideal time to facilitate feelings of desire and desirability. Just as with bridges to desire, you can develop his, hers, and ours afterplay scenarios that enhance the role and meaning of your couple sexual style.

Exercise: Your Orgasmic and Afterplay Scenarios

Each couple can develop a unique style of sharing orgasm, as well as sharing afterplay. Just as there is no one right orgasmic pattern, there is no correct afterplay scenario. It is important to develop your own style of afterplay, share it with your partner, be accepting rather than competitive, and enjoy each other's orgasmic scenarios and preferences.

In this exercise, we suggest that the man share with his partner how he experiences and feels about his orgasmic pattern. He should make at least one request to try something new to enhance orgasmic pleasure. The woman then takes her turn to share her experiences and feelings about her orgasmic pattern and make at least one request to enhance orgasmic pleasure. It is important to share with your partner your personal history and feelings about orgasmic discoveries and learnings. As a sexual culture we go from one extreme to another. For women, the original extreme was silence and ignorance about female orgasm. The new extreme is to set competitive, performance-oriented orgasm goals. The search is on for the perfect orgasm—being orgasmic each time, being multi-orgasmic, orgasm as the ultimate satisfaction, the "G-spot" orgasm. How has this affected you as a woman and a couple? Identify your preferred orgasmic response pattern and share it with your partner. He needs to accept your orgasm voice rather than trying to change it to meet some performance myth. You are responsible for your orgasm, not him.

During these encounters, transition from sensual pleasure to erotic stimulation when you feel receptive and responsive rather than trying to move at your partner's pace. Allow yourself to be "selfish" and take in pleasure. As your subjective arousal builds toward 6 or 7, you can choose whether to stay with erotic flow using manual, oral, or rubbing stimulation to orgasm or to transition to intercourse. Either way, feel free to use all the erotic techniques to enhance erotic flow. These include multiple stimulation, loving or erotic talk, erotic fantasies, and "orgasm triggers." Do you prefer a predictable or variable orgasmic pattern(s)? Enjoy it for yourself and share this with your partner.

Together, talk about your afterplay experiences. How satisfied are you with you afterplay scenarios—do they enhance bonding and satisfaction? We suggest each of you make at least one request to play out a new afterplay scenario or technique. You could experiment with a new, cuddly position; share your emotional, romantic, or erotic couple memories; savor the moment non-verbally, play a silly touching game, share a glass of wine and a treat, take a shower and wash each other, go for a walk or run, read aloud from your favorite book of poetry. You want afterplay to be a positive, integral component of your couple sexual style.

Closing Thoughts

We hope you have developed a new, more positive, and realistic understanding of the role and meaning of orgasm, as well as the meaning and function of afterplay. Orgasm is not a performance test but an integral part of the desire, pleasure, arousal, erotic flow process. Be aware that female orgasmic response is more variable and flexible than male orgasm. This is not a matter of better or worse, but a way to understand and celebrate differences. Afterplay is an ideal milieu in which to share and enhance couple sexual satisfaction. If you want to enhance the sexual experience, enlist your partner, who can be your intimate, erotic friend and help you increase pleasure, orgasm, and satisfaction.

PART **III**

Surmounting Sexual Challenges

CHAPTER **10**

Overcoming Sexual Inhibitions

Couples find this a very difficult topic to approach. Inhibitions, fears, depression, alcohol or drug abuse, shame about sexual trauma, and self-consciousness are "poisons" that subvert healthy couple sexuality. One way or another (couple sex therapy is an excellent resource) you can confront these very difficult issues. If you don't, the inhibitions can become chronic, severe, and controlling. The inhibitions will poison not only your sexual relationship but will subvert your entire relationship, robbing it of intimacy and satisfaction.

We will help you understand and change these poisons so you can have a freer, more satisfying intimate relationship. The change process involves taking personal responsibility for your sexuality. Your partner cannot do it for you, but as part of your intimate sexual team he/she can be your "partner in healing" to establish a comfortable, satisfying individual and couple sexuality.

Recognizing Inhibitions

What is the most common inhibition/poison? It is self-consciousness. Whether based on a negative body image, guilt or shame, sexual anxiety, inhibition about pleasure or eroticism, fear of performance pressure, or sexual obsessions, sexual self-consciousness subverts the comfort/pleasure/ eroticism process. What is the most significant emotional inhibition? It is anger. Whether about the past or present, individual or relationship anger subverts healthy sexuality. What is the most difficult psychological issue? It is dealing with past negative sexual experiences and developing a sense of deserving pleasure in your current sexual relationship.

You need to understand and confront these inhibitions so they do not control your sexual self-esteem and couple sexuality. You owe it to yourself and your relationship to be a healthy sexual adult. When we talk to couples who feel stuck in their poisons, we try to motivate them by telling them that their parents might not have been a good marital or sexual model, but they owe it to their children to be a good marital and sexual model for them. Take pride in ending the cycle of sexual unhappiness and dysfunction. You want sexuality to play a healthy 15–20% role in your life and relationship.

Although the potential for desire and pleasure is natural for both women and men, it is very vulnerable and easy to kill. You can't treat inhibitions with benign neglect; they will worsen over time. Now is the time to confront and change the poisons, so let's get started.

Anger   Anger can have an extremely corrosive effect on couple sexuality. Chronic conflict and anger subvert your emotional bond. The partner is no longer your trusted, intimate friend but an untrustworthy critic who could hurt or even destroy you. Why would you want to sleep with the enemy?

Feeling hurt or put down is the main precursor to anger. This feeling is especially poisonous if the hurt/anger involves your body image or sexuality. For example, a woman intent on hurting her husband complains that his penis is smaller than an ex-boyfriend's. When the anger dissipates, she is regretful and apologetic, but the injured partner continues to ruminate and feel put-down. The cycle of hurt–anger–alienation continues to build and becomes controlling. Anger destroys intimacy and fuels sexual avoidance.

"Intimate coercion" is a common cause of anger, as well as inhibited female sexual desire. The man pushing sex and threatening negative consequences if the woman does not go along is an example of winning a sex battle but losing an intimate relationship. Intimate coercion is a demand for sex at this time and in this way regardless of your partner's feelings and needs. This demand, if not met, will result in negative consequences such as harassment, public put-downs, or withholding money or help with the children or household tasks. Men and women view intimate coercion dramatically differently. He denies the pattern or says it's her fault and is baffled by her anger. She sees him as mean and controlling, with his sexual needs overriding her emotional needs. Intimate coercion must be confronted and this couple poison eliminated.

A common source of anger stems from the hurt and violation of trust surrounding an extra-marital affair. Although men have twice as many affairs as women (and unmarried couples have more affairs than married couples), it is usually the man who reacts with greater anger. A female affair is the reverse of the traditional double standard. Even if the affair is over, the partner feels insecure and judged; this is usually expressed as anger.

Some men react by shutting down sexually, while others forcefully initiate sex as if to avenge the affair. Anger sex alienates the woman and kills loving feelings. Typically, the woman's reaction to discovering the man's affair is angry withdrawal. This anger can build a wall of resentment that shuts out touching and caring. Anger and alienation build on themselves and poison the relationship, especially sexual desire.

Sexual issues are not the chief reason for couple anger. More commonly, the causes are hurt, disappointment, frustration with the partner, or inability to resolve an issue. Hurt is caused by the partner saying derogatory things about you in public or in front of the children, revealing a sensitive or secret problem he/she had promised to honor, telling a joke at the partner's expense, or reneging on an emotional or financial agreement. Disappointment includes finding that the partner lied about his academic or professional credentials, learning that the woman's family is not as loving and accepting as promised, that time together has been usurped by compulsive TV watching, and promises of emotional and sexual intimacy have been substituted with a marginal marriage. Hurt, disappointment, and frustration evolve into anger.

How do you deal with anger so it no longer controls your relationship? First, be aware that anger is usually a secondary emotion. You need to address the primary emotions of hurt or disappointment. Negative emotions are best dealt with outside the bedroom. Talk out issues on a walk, over the kitchen table, in a therapist's office. You can learn from the past, but you cannot change the past. You do not want your life and relationship held hostage to past hurt or anger.

What do you need to do and what do you need from your partner to successfully resolve the anger? Resolution doesn't mean forgetting or pretending. Rather, resolution means processing the hurt/disappointment issues and feelings and determining what you can do in the present to eliminate the poison. The most common outcome is that the partner takes responsibility and apologizes for the hurt, which was real but usually not intentional. In giving and accepting the apology, the commitment between the partners is that they do not repeat the pattern. They are then free to pursue a healthy intimate relationship.

Guilt and Shame   Guilt and shame are the most self-defeating of emotions. In couple relations they are especially likely to revolve around past abusive, emotionally traumatic, or sexual incidents. When you feel guilty, you lower your self-esteem and are more vulnerable to being re-victimized or to repeat the same destructive behavior. Shame is all-encompassing. You are not just guilty about a specific incident, but your whole sense of self is shame-based. An example is the woman who feels guilty about a sexual experience with a youth minister when she was 10 and he 21. At 21, she is devastated by a date rape incident. This is an example of a re-victimization, which further lowers her self-esteem and increases her sense of guilt and shame. Another example of the self-defeating nature of guilt is a man who spends $65 for manual stimulation to orgasm at a massage parlor. He keeps this secret and avoids his wife both emotionally and sexually. He is afraid that if she knew he engaged in paid sex she'd think he was "scum." As his self-esteem is lowered, he feels more guilty and lonely, returns to the massage parlor, and the self-defeating shame cycle continues.

Guilt and shame have no positive function for the person or relationship. Guilt results in isolation, lowered self-esteem, and reinforces self-defeating emotional and sexual behaviors. The key in confronting guilt is to stop "blaming the victim." Especially in child sexual abuse, it is the perpetrator who is responsible, not the child. The key to processing this as an adult is to realize that the core of sexual abuse is that the adult's sexual needs override the child's emotional needs. With guilt, the adult views the abuse as her "shameful secret."

It is very important to realize that males can be sexually, as well as emotionally and physically, abused. Men feel even more guilty and shameful since it's usually a male perpetrator. Abuse is not supposed to happen to males. Sadly, men hide and avoid processing traumatic experiences, which result in emotional and sexual impairment. The male does not even share his abuse history with his partner; it is his "shameful secret."

The key to dealing with past negative or traumatic incidents is to confront and process these experiences in a safe, supportive relationship. This can include individual, couple, or group therapy, or a self-help group. Accept that it was not your fault. It need not be a shameful secret or a controlling life event. Process thoughts, feelings, and learnings both in retrospect and now. Adopt the self-view of being a "survivor," not a "victim," and implement the mantra "living well is the best revenge."

In situations where you feel guilty because of your negative behavior, you need to take responsibility for the behavior, apologize, and, if possible, make amends. Most important, adopt healthy emotional and sexual behaviors and use all your resources to ensure that the negative behavior does not recur. Shame subverts this process. In truth, you deserve to have sexuality play a healthy role in your current life and relationship.

Anxiety and Inhibitions   Sex and pleasure belong together. However, the association of sex and performance results in anticipatory and/or performance anxiety. Approaching sex with anxiety, fear of failure, a wish to procrastinate or avoid, fear of embarrassment, or wanting to get it over with are turn-offs for both partners. Performance anxiety emphasizes sex as a pass–fail test in which any problem cues a fear of failure—fear that controls the experience. A performance orientation causes increased anxiety and subverts desire and pleasure.

Inhibitions—which include psychological, relational, and physical factors—rob sex of vitality and playfulness and block pleasure. Inhibitions interfere with the natural progression of comfort, desire, arousal, erotic flow, and satisfaction. Common inhibitions include poor body image, reluctance to initiate, unwillingness to let go sexually, embarrassment about nudity, fear of making sexual requests or disclosing turn-ons, reluctance to try an erotic scenario, embarrassment, and self-consciousness. Inhibitions take the fun out of sex and result in rigid sex roles and behavior. They are a psychological form of withholding. You are not free with yourself, your partner, or couple sexuality. Rather than sexuality being open, flowing, and free, it is guarded, mechanical, and mediocre.

Obsessions and compulsions are another type of inhibition. Sometimes these are part of an obsessive–compulsive disorder, but more commonly they are specific to sex. The best example is the man who has a secret fetish arousal pattern that controls couple sexuality. The woman mistakenly feels it must reflect something negative about her sexuality and desirability. Another example is the woman who insists on compulsive, ritualistic washing of genitals before sex, resulting in loss of erotic feelings. Other types of compulsive behavior are the man counting intercourse strokes, the woman insisting on using three forms of birth control or immediately jumping up after intercourse to douche.

Obsessive–compulsive behavior is an irrational anxiety that views sex and genitals as dirty or dangerous. The key to breaking the hold of sexual obsessions and compulsions is to be aware that these are irrational, self-defeating ways to manage anxiety; in fact, in the long run they only serve to increase anxiety. Working as an intimate team, you need to confront these negative patterns and experience the freedom of sexual comfort and pleasure.

Confronting and Changing Inhibitions

Recognizing an inhibition and being willing to address the sexual poison is the first step in attaining sexual freedom. Do not be dissuaded by feelings of embarrassment, shame, or stigma. Awareness is power. Your partner can be your ally in freeing your relationship from poisons and sharing the joys of intimacy and eroticism. View inhibitions as "traps" that you need to confront rather than deny or minimize.

The challenge for you and your partner is to replace the poison with sexually healthy ways of thinking, behaving, and feeling. A good example is the person (usually the woman, but often the man) who feels guilty or damaged by child sexual abuse. Rather than keeping this a shameful secret or feeling like an anxious/angry victim, process the experience with your mate and ask him/her to be your "partner in healing." When you are able to experience desire, arousal, orgasm, and satisfaction in the context of an open, equitable, trusting relationship, you realize that you deserve to be a survivor and that "living well is the best revenge." This includes your right and ability to veto anything aversive and trust that your partner will honor your veto. Unless you can say "no" to sex, you're not free to say "yes" to healthy couple sexuality.

Another example is the man with a compulsive fetish who acts out on an Internet sex site. He is controlled by the secrecy, shame, and eroticism. When his partner discovers he spends more than $600 per month on Internet sex, she is angry and he is ashamed. Rather than avoiding the problem, he needs to share the impact of this poison so it is recognized rather than hidden. The poison must be challenged. The one-two combination is to confront and eliminate the poison and to build an intimate, erotic couple sexuality.

Poisons thrive on secrecy. The best way to prevent a "lapse" from becoming a "relapse" is to share the information with your partner within 24 hours so that it does not become a shameful secret that propels you into a guilt/acting-out cycle. The sexual cover-up is even more damaging than the incident. Rather than hiding out, the couple is urged to initiate an intimate pleasuring date within the next one to three days. The poison cannot be allowed to reassert control over self-esteem or couple sexuality. Healthy sexuality is facilitated by sharing, and subverted by guilt, shame, and secrecy.

Penny and Jason   Penny and Jason are a strikingly attractive couple in their early 30s. Relatives and friends were envious of their "perfect" life. Well-educated, athletic, and social, the couple lived in a stylish condo in a regentrified section of the city. Sadly, the reality of their sexual life was totally at odds with external appearances. They had been a romantic love/passionate sex couple for the first seven months, but once they were a committed couple, the poisons/inhibitions took over.

Jason had not disclosed his "sexual demon," which was a compulsive pattern to masturbate to Internet videos showing two or more women engaging in cunnilingus. He had masturbated exclusively to this scenario on a daily basis for six or seven years, checking many different sites but increasingly using two paid sites. He was spending between $700 and $1,200 per month on Internet sex. This was Jason's shameful secret, and he was very fearful of anyone, especially Penny, discovering this.

Penny and Jason naively hoped that with love and commitment she would finally leave behind her "sexual demon," the emotional conflict she felt about two date rape experiences. One occurred with an older cousin when she was 15 and the other at 22 at a college graduation party. She had processed this with friends, sister and mother, her minister, individual and group therapists—everyone except a male, including Jason. Penny was fearful of Jason's judgment.

When talking with each other and confidantes about whether to marry, their focus was on fear of commitment. They danced around the sexuality issues. Their parents and minister strongly urged them to commit to marriage with the promise that marriage would solve any problem. Although we are pro-marriage, we acknowledge that marriage in itself does not resolve poisons/inhibitions.

As often happens, the issue was brought to the table by a discovery, leading to a crisis. Both Jason and Penny were financially knowledgeable, prudent people. Most of their income was in a joint account, but each spouse had $500 a month in personal discretionary spending. Penny could not understand why Jason was always broke. In trying to be helpful, Penny discovered his pattern of monthly online payments to an account she had never heard of. Being a computer sophisticated individual, she discovered it was a porn site. When Penny clicked on it, she felt both repulsed and intimidated by the blatant eroticism that clearly played to a male porn fantasy—women being sexual with other women. When confronted, Jason was humiliated and reacted aggressively by attacking Penny as the "sexual police." He blamed her for his Internet misuse by saying she had pulled a "bait and switch" about sex. She pretended to love him and to be sexual, but she was manipulative and "frigid." Penny felt attacked and betrayed, similar to feelings she had experienced after the date rape. The cycle of blame–counterblame became extremely vicious. The minister, whom they liked and respected, counseled forgiveness and prayer. While this is supportive guidance, the issues surrounding the shame-making poisons needed to be processed in a therapeutic manner.

A referral to a marital therapist with a sub-specialty in sexuality was a very wise decision. Penny and Jason were feeling wounded, bitter, and almost hopeless when they arrived in the therapist's office. The therapist realized there was a new poison in the system—the accusations/counterattack cycle that needed to stop immediately. In the individual psychological/relational/sexual history sessions, Jason and Penny disclosed the true story of the sexual vulnerabilities and secrets that had burdened them. In the couple feedback session, the therapist was emotionally supportive but also confrontational about the need for them to understand and deal with these hard issues individually and as a couple. Jason agreed to join a Sex Addicts Anonymous group and have a blocking system to eliminate these sex sites. Most important, he committed to a transparency agreement with Penny. She could be his ally in confronting the compulsive fetish pattern.

In a couple change program, it is crucial that the partners not engage in "tit-for-tat" agreements. Each person needs to commit to changing his/her poison and be supportive of the partner. Do not fall into the trap that if the partner doesn't change, then you won't either. Penny needed to disclose her wounded self-esteem and date rape history and turn to Jason as her "partner in healing." The challenge for Penny (and the couple) was to integrate emotional intimacy (safety and acceptance) with eroticism (letting go and enjoying the intensity of sexuality) in this marriage. The therapist observed that this would be a challenge even without the drama of the discovery and the couple attack–counterattack reaction. Penny and Jason owed it to themselves and their marriage to address the poisons and to rebuild couple trust and sexuality. Instead of hiding behind the perfect couple image, they needed to be emotionally open and trust that their spouse would be an ally in addressing these difficult issues.

It was not an easy process, but Jason found that with the sexual compulsivity out of his life he was a better person, a better spouse, and better able to be Penny's intimate partner and ally. For the first time since adolescence, Penny felt like a "survivor," not a "victim." She felt affirmed that Jason respected her emotional and sexual feelings. This allowed Penny and Jason to integrate intimacy and eroticism into their couple sexual style. Sexuality was now a positive resource in the marriage, not an area of secrecy and shame.

What Poisons Sexual Desire?

As we have noted, sexual desire is surprisingly easy to subvert. Inhibitions and secrecy eventually will kill sexual desire. At a minimum you need to get the poison and secrecy out of your sexual life. Ideally you will totally overcome the inhibition. For many people a more realistic goal is to modify your sexual attitudes and behavior so that the inhibition no longer controls couple sexuality. Poisons do not deserve power over your life or couple sex. The inhibitions and negative feelings might not disappear, but you can break their power.

Inability to accept the reality of past traumas—an abortion, affair, humiliation, shame—should not be allowed to control self-esteem. Take responsibility for yourself in the present. You cannot change the past, but you can learn from it so it does not control your current and future sexuality. Be a survivor who is aware of the poisons/inhibitions and is committed to not repeating self-defeating behavior. You are empowered to acknowledge sexuality as an integral part of your personality, and express sexuality so it contributes a positive 15–20% to your life and intimate relationship.

Exercise: Confronting Your Personal Inhibitions and Enlisting Your Partner as Your Intimate Ally

This is the most difficult exercise in the book. We ask you to identify your personal inhibitions/poisons and share these with your partner. In this way, you break their hold over you and your relationship, and replace it with a comfortable, growing, and vital couple sexuality.

Some people decide the best way to share this sensitive material is through a face-to-face talk; others choose sharing through a letter, and some with the help of a couple therapist. Do what is comfortable and right for you, but do it. Don't continue the secrecy and avoidance.

Be empathic, respectful, and supportive of your partner. The worst outcome is using this disclosure in a hostile, put-down manner. Remember, the focus is on the present—freeing you for intimate, vital couple sexuality. People maintain secrecy and poisons from fear of judgment or stigma. Do you trust yourself and your partner enough to challenge the status quo? Be clear why you are sharing this sensitive material and what you request of your partner. Make sure your partner is open and able to be an ally in healing.

Also be clear what you want to experience emotionally and sexually in freeing your couple sexual style from the poison. Tell your partner at least two things you want to change. The key to change is approaching sexuality from the perspective of each person taking responsibility for her/his sexuality and feeling and acting as an intimate team. Be specific about what you will do individually and as a couple to promote change and work toward gradual change. No change plan is perfect, but it will be successful if it is based on clear, positive, realistic (non-perfectionistic) goals. Be willing to problem solve when you encounter difficulties so you stay on the same team. As you process successes and setbacks, remember that change is a couple task and that sexuality is a shared, intimate process. If a poison/inhibition reappears, don't pretend you are not frustrated and disappointed. Just keep the focus on eliminating or reducing the power of the inhibition. Put your energy into enjoying vital, resilient couple sexuality.

If you find you cannot successfully do this on your own, make a wise decision to seek out a couple therapist with a sub-specialty in sexual function and dysfunction. Suggested resources are listed in Appendix A.

Closing Thoughts

There are a myriad of emotional and sexual poisons/inhibitions, both past and in the present, that can subvert your sexuality. When poisons are identified and confronted, they lose power. By assuming responsibility for your inhibitions, sharing with your partner as your intimate ally, and working together to get the poison out of your couple sexual relationship, you ensure that change is well on the way. Successfully confronting the poisons becomes a source of pride.

Removing inhibitions is necessary, but not sufficient, for revitalizing couple sexuality. You need to develop a new couple sexual style of intimacy, pleasuring, and eroticism. Turn to each other to monitor poisons and ensure that a lapse does not turn into a relapse because of secrecy and avoidance. Enjoy a range of sexual experiences and meanings. The best way to ensure sexual health is to continue to devote the time and energy needed to grow your intimate, erotic relationship.

CHAPTER 11

Dealing with Illness and Sex

When your body is healthy and functional, you take it for granted. People think little about health until they experience an illness or disability. Sexual response is anchored in your physical body. Illness can affect you in every part of your life, sex included. The good news is that illness does not stop you from being sexual. The bad news is that you have to adapt to your body changes (including side effects of medications) if you are to maintain healthy individual and couple sexuality.

The three biological/physical systems that directly effect sexuality are the vascular, neurological, and hormonal systems. Of these the vascular system is the most frequently affected, whether by high blood pressure or negative health habits such as drinking or smoking. As people age, their neurological and vascular systems become less efficient, and they become more prone to illness. Paradoxically, it is the side effects of medications used to treat common illnesses, whether high blood pressure or depression, that is the number one culprit in physiologically based sexual problems.

We are strong advocates for the psychobiosocial (the politically correct term is "biopsychosocial") model of understanding, assessing, treating, and preventing a relapse of sexual dysfunction. You need to attend to all the causes and dimensions of your sexual dysfunction to truly understand its role in interfering with your couple sexual style. So, for example, although hormonal functioning is the most stable and the least likely to cause sexual problems, if hormonal function is significantly impaired—e.g., through surgery for uterine cancer or a pituitary gland disease—it must be addressed. In addressing illness/disability factors you need to consider (1) whether the illness is acute or chronic, (2) side-effects of medications—both prescribed and over the counter and (3) health habits that can subvert your physical well-being. Anything that negatively impacts your physical body can negatively impact your sexual health and response.

Traditionally, the role of psychological factors in physical and sexual health has been misunderstood. Rather than applying an integrative, psychobiosocial model, people still think of the mind/body dichotomy. "It's all in your head" dismisses the problem and blames the person. The old view, especially of female pain during intercourse and male erectile dysfunction, was that 90% was caused by psychological or relationship factors, for which the answer was individual or couple/sex therapy. The new view is that 95% of sexual problems are caused by physiological/medical factors and that the answer is to treat the individual with a stand-alone medical intervention. As a culture we go from one extreme to another, looking for simple answers and simple cures. The sexual truth is that problems are usually multi-causal and multi-dimensional, requiring an integrated, comprehensive couple approach.

One of the most helpful suggestions is to schedule an appointment with your internist or medical specialist. Most physicians only see patients individually and do not raise sexual issues, much less provide sexual information or offer sexual counseling. Make it clear to the doctor that you as a couple want to understand the illness. Be an active patient; discuss medications and their sexual side-effects, and what changes in health habits would promote physical and sexual health. You are seeking medical and health guidance, not sexual counseling. Doing this as a couple can bring out the most attentive, helpful aspect of the physician.

Physicians are not well-trained in sexual medicine and worry about overstepping privacy or value boundaries. Medicine is at its best when there is an acute problem, a specific diagnosis, and a specific medical intervention. Unfortunately, this is not the reality for sex problems. The psychobiosocial approach is a more relevant model. Very important resources when dealing with illness, medications, and health behaviors include being an active, knowledgeable patient; understanding the impact of the disease and treatment on individual and couple sexuality; and determining what medical and health behaviors you can change to improve sexual function. If your physician is not comfortable or able to play a helpful role, do not hesitate to ask for a referral to a sexual medicine specialist or to a couple sex therapist. (See Appendix A and Appendix B.)

Amanda and Trevor   Amanda remembers her 87-year-old mother telling her that "aging isn't for wimps." Amanda at 62 and Trevor at 65 were dealing with a number of medical issues but were committed to maintaining healthy couple sexuality. Part of their confidence came from having successfully dealt with Amanda's breast cancer at 42 and Trevor's recovery from a car accident at 55. Their mantra was to be active patients and to use all their medical and health resources to deal with the problems, not let medical problems define their lives or their sexuality.

Amanda had done monthly breast self-exams since her early 20s. When she noticed a lump, she immediately contacted her gynecologist, followed up with a mammogram, had a biopsy, and chose a well-respected breast surgeon. Cancer is a disease of timing, and early detection and a comprehensive treatment protocol was life-saving for Amanda. Twenty years later she is still rigorous about her monthly self-exams and a yearly mammogram.

Trevor's car had been rear-ended by a speeding, drunken driver ten years previously. He had his seat belt on, and the air-bag reduced the impact damage. The hardest thing for Trevor was not the surgery and hospitalization, but following the rehabilitation and physical therapy protocol. Amanda strongly supported Trevor physically and emotionally. Although he wasn't a perfect patient, the physical therapist said he was doing a fine job in rehabilitation. Trevor accepted that his left arm would not return to pre-accident use and that he was left with a minor limp. As Amanda and their friends said, it could have been much worse.

Physical intimacy was a positive resource in coping with their medical crises. As is the case with approximately 50% of women, breast stimulation had not been an integral part of Amanda's sexual response pattern. After the cancer treatment, she requested that Trevor not engage in direct breast stimulation with either breast, a request that he honored. A benefit was that both manual stimulation and rubbing (especially with Amanda being active) became a prominent form of sexual stimulation. After the accident, Trevor learned to accept sensual, non-genital massage as both healing and relaxing.

Now in their 60s, both were taking medications for blood pressure. Trevor used medication to control his cholesterol and diabetes and Amanda for arthritis, especially in her back and hands. They were good patients and had two couple consultations with their internist about their illnesses and sexuality. They found her easier to talk to and more accessible than the specialists. The internist suggested that they plan sexual activities around times Amanda experienced the least pain and most mobility. This was before 9 o'clock in the morning after taking her pain medication and exercising by walking.

The internist urged both Trevor and Amanda to be rigorous in following their medication protocol. This was particularly difficult for Trevor, who did not like taking pills. However, after keeping a diary for a month he realized how much better his numbers were when he followed the medication regimen. The internist also urged Trevor to use Cialis each Saturday morning. She explained that Cialis did not give him an automatic erection but did reduce anticipatory anxiety about intercourse. When Trevor was open to Amanda's stimulation and felt subjectively aroused, the pro-erection medication compensated for the effects of the illnesses and medications, improving the efficacy of his vascular system. Trevor felt more secure in maintaining his erection during intercourse.

As they talked afterward, Amanda emphasized two factors. Most important, she wanted to share intimacy and touching with Trevor and maintain a couple sexual life. Too many of her female friends had given up sexual intimacy because their husbands or boyfriends had become embarrassed and frustrated with erectile problems and just withdrew. Amanda and Trevor were aware that because they were older and dealing with health issues, they needed to be flexible and accepting, not feel they owed each other a sexual performance, intercourse, or orgasm each time. In addition, Amanda asked that Trevor not apologize for himself if the sexual encounter did not include intercourse; nor did she want him to feel rejected if the pain blocked her sexual desire. Amanda enjoyed anticipating sex, but did not want to feel pressure to perform or prove something to Trevor.

Trevor admitted that he'd always considered sex his domain, and it felt strange to have a female physician as well as Amanda urging him on sexually. His biggest concern was what to do when his penis wasn't "strong enough" for intercourse. For the past 30 years, he'd enjoyed Amanda stimulating him to orgasm when she wasn't interested in intercourse, a scenario that had been good for both of them. This had evolved from experience rather than talking about it. Trevor worried that "talking sex to death" would kill his desire and confidence. Amanda agreed and assured him it was great if the sexual encounter did not proceed to intercourse. They could transition to erotic, non-intercourse sex or a cuddly, sensual scenario.

Trevor's other concern was becoming dependent on medication for everything—including sex. Amanda reminded him that the internist suggested they focus on enjoying both intercourse and erotic, non-intercourse sex. Many couples eventually fade out the pro-erection medication, using it as a back-up to ensure that performance anxiety is not resensitized. Trevor would use Cialis if the last three encounters had not progressed to intercourse.

Trevor and Amanda's joint commitment was to deal realistically and positively with their illnesses and medications. They hoped to enjoy life into their 70s and 80s and didn't want their life plans subverted by physical health factors. Maintaining a healthy physical body was reinforced by their desire to maintain couple intimacy and vital sexuality. Trevor loved the idea of beating the odds and enjoying sex into his 80s since he'd always been a competitive guy. Amanda realized that with illnesses, medications, and aging they needed each other more sexually. She was really enjoying this new chapter in their couple sexual style. Trevor acknowledged that "good enough" sex fit their current life and health status, and that they could thrive recreationally and sexually in this life phase.

Chronic Illness and Caretaking

This is a particularly complex and sensitive topic. Whether the chronic ill-ness is multiple sclerosis, Alzheimer's, cancer, kidney dialysis, debilitating arthritis, or chronic pain, when the spouse assumes a caretaking role this affects couple intimacy and sexuality. Dealing with incontinence, dress-ing, and personal hygiene can cause you to de-eroticize your spouse. You needn't be ashamed of this reality.

Couples who define intimacy and sexuality broadly and flexibly find there does not have to be a split around caretaking and sexuality. Acceptance that the essence of sexuality is giving and receiving pleasure-oriented touch is the core concept. Whether the healing touch involves holding hands during a medical procedure or giving a body massage for pain reduction, touch can bond you as a couple as you deal with the illness. Touch can also promote a sensual/playful way of sharing pleasure whether lying and stroking each other or taking a bath together. Sometimes pleasurable touch is mutual, sometimes you take turns, and at other times it can be one-way stimula-tion. When dealing with the reality of illness, openness to variable, flexible sexuality is crucial. This is especially true when speaking of erotic, non-intercourse sex. With manual, oral, and rubbing stimulation couples can use aides both to increase comfort (being sexual on a foam mat) and to increase arousal/orgasm (use of vibrator stimulation).

Illness and disability can alter intercourse—especially positions and intercourse movements. Clinging to traditional man-on-top intercourse will disrupt your sexuality if the woman has a hip replacement, experi-ences leg pain, or the man has heart/breathing problems or knee pain. The key is to accept the illness/disability and incorporate a variable, flex-ible approach to intercourse positions and movements. Adopting the Good Enough Sex model allows you the freedom to enjoy a range of sensual and sexual experiences. Don't play the "if only" game about either your ill-ness or your sexuality. Accept the reality of your illness/disability, includ-ing needing help or caretaking from your partner. This is part of your life together, but it cannot become your self-definition as a couple. Your ill-ness/disability is an integral part of you, but it need not control or define you. You can enjoy couple intimacy and sexuality separate from issues of illness and caretaking.

Exercise: Acceptance and Coping With Illness While Maintaining Healthy Intimacy and Sexuality

There are two parts to this exercise. First, increase your understanding and acceptance of your illness/disability/medications. The person with the illness commits to increasing information by exploring trustworthy websites or going to an illness-specific support group. The partner agrees to consult helper/caretaker websites and attend a support group to increase awareness and learn helpful vs. subverting coping strategies. You can share information about the illness, medications, and resources, and develop both cognitive and emotional understanding. Schedule an appointment as a couple with your general physician or specialist to clarify medical, medication, and health behaviors that promote physical and sexual well-being. Agree on at least three questions to ask. We suggest writing them down and handing this to the physician. The more knowledge you receive as a patient, the better. You want to be an active, involved patient so you can advocate for yourself and enhance your physical health.

The second part of the exercise asks you to positively incorporate what you've learned into your couple sexual style. What are the specific physical or medication vulnerabilities you need to actively compensate for? Remember, the psychobiosocial model. Use all your psychological, medical, couple, and psychosexual skill resources to address and change any vulnerabilities. Don't just make a list; actually implement these changes. Try a different time to be sexual, adopt a different pleasuring/erotic scenario, use a lubricant as part of the pleasuring process, use a pro-erection medication, try a different intercourse position, work cooperatively to facilitate intromission, use pillows or a futon to facilitate comfort, or use a vibrator to transition from arousal to orgasm. Be comfortable taking a break and then returning to intercourse. Do not let the illness control your individual and couple sexuality. Do what is helpful to establish a variable, flexible couple sexual style that honors the reality of the illness. Make these guidelines and techniques as personal and concrete as possible.

Closing Thoughts

The core guideline of this chapter is that an illness/disability does not stop you from being sexual, but it does alter your individual and couple sexual response pattern. This awareness needs to be integrated into your body image and sexual self-esteem. Do not allow the illness or disability to control individual or couple sexuality. We encourage you to adopt the psychobiosocial approach to understanding your sexual body. Don't be trapped in the perfect body/perfect sexual performance myth. Feel free to use all your resources to develop a comfortable, functional couple sexual style. Accept your physical and sexual limitations, adopt the Good Enough Sex model, and see yourselves as intimate and erotic friends who share sexual pleasure and sexual response.

CHAPTER **12**

Looking for Help from
Pro-Sex Medications

With the introduction of Viagra in 1998, there was a revolution involving the origin and treatment of sexual problems. The prior belief was that sexual problems were caused by psychological or relational factors. Since 1998, the pendulum has swung to the opposite extreme. Sexual dysfunction (especially for males) is viewed as a medical/physical problem, with the emphasis on finding the right medical treatment. Women hope that medical science will develop a female equivalent of Viagra for desire, arousal, and orgasm problems. "Better living through chemistry" has swept the sexual field.

When it comes to pro-erection medication (Viagra, Levitra, and Cialis) ads on TV, the message is clear. Take this pill and it will return you to the totally predictable and easy erections of your teen years. The second message is that your erections will again be autonomous; you need nothing from your partner except her urging you to talk to your doctor. It's a very upbeat and seductive marketing message. Many men skip the medical step and get the medication directly from Internet sites.

What is the reality of pro-erection medications for male and couple sexuality? The good news first. Viagra, Levitra, and Cialis are safe and effective drugs for the great majority of males. They improve the efficacy of your vascular system and reduce anticipatory anxiety. Men who had avoided intercourse because of performance anxiety and the embarrassment of failure are again engaging in couple sex. Although there are individual and couple differences, the typical man experiences successful intercourse during 65–85% of encounters when using a pro-erection medication.

The problem is that the 65–85% successful intercourse rate does not match the teenage and young adult sexual model or the promises of the marketing ads. So the man is embarrassed that he's a "Viagra failure." This negative emotion and stigma cause him to avoid any sexual contact. If he can't achieve 100% predictable erection and intercourse performance, he makes a unilateral, non-verbal decision to stop being sexual. When it's "intercourse or nothing," nothing eventually wins. Viagra has probably caused more non-sexual relationships than anything else in history. This is not because it's a failed drug, but because it's touted as a stand-alone medical intervention; its marketing overpromise of a return to the totally predictable, autonomous erections of your youth sets you up for failure.

Pro-erection medications can break the cycle of avoidance by serving as a cue to initiate sex, promoting the efficacy of your vascular system, and facilitating enjoyment of intercourse again. The key to successful use is to accept the Good Enough Sex approach to male and couple sexuality. To use such medication in an optimal manner, the man (and couple) needs to adopt two core guidelines. First, the medication should be integrated into your couple style of intimacy, pleasuring, and eroticism. Don't treat it as a "magic pill," stand-alone intervention. The truth is that sexuality is an intimate, interactive, interpersonal experience, not an autonomous one. You are a sexual person/couple, not a performance machine.

We also stress the importance of having positive, realistic sexual expectations. The rigid requirement of a 100% perfect erection and intercourse performance dooms the couple to eventual erectile dysfunction and avoidance. The 85% criterion of Good Enough Sex is the healthy approach for male and couple sexuality. When sex does not flow into intercourse, you transition (without apology or self-consciousness) to either an erotic, non-intercourse scenario or a cuddly, sensual scenario. Accept that in the most loving, sexual couples 5–15% of encounters are dissatisfying or dysfunctional. Sexual variability and flexibility is normal; it need not be a cause for anxiety or worry.

Pro-sex medications can be a positive resource for your couple sexuality, especially to counteract the side-effects of illness and medications. The hope is that in the next 5–10 years, medical research will develop a better range of medications to facilitate sexual functioning for both women and men. These are crucial resources for sexual function, but you can't ask a drug to do it all. Rather than view the medications as a stand-alone intervention, they need to be integrated into your couple style of intimacy, pleasuring, and eroticism.

The best way to understand sexuality is as a couple psychobiosocial process. Psychologically, you need to value sexuality for yourself and your relationship. Developing an intimate, interactive couple sexual style is a healthy challenge. Don't fall into the trap of hoping that the medication will return you to the easy, predictable erections you experienced in a new relationship in your 20s. Remember the key guidelines, which are to maintain positive, realistic (not perfect or "magic") expectations and integrate the medication into your couple sexual style.

Roger and Celia   Other than during the first year of their relationship, sex had been problematic for Celia and Roger. Now in their mid-50s, they last year they launched the last of their four children into her own job and apartment. They see themselves as loving, committed partners who enjoy their lives, marriage, and especially parenting. Their two older children are married, and Roger and Celia hope in a couple of years to be grandparents, a role they very much look forward to. During the parenting years, sex slid into a weekend night routine with a frequency of 2–4 times a month. Sex was functional, but unremarkable, a relatively unimportant part of their marriage.

Roger's first erectile problem occurred in his late 30s. He attributed that incident to fatigue and worry about the academic problems of his oldest son. Celia was not concerned about his loss of erection and tried to reassure Roger that all she needed was to feel close. Over the next few years, erectile problems occurred intermittently—about once a month. However, at age 48, the frequency of Roger's erectile problems increased, and by age 50 there were more erectile failures than successful intercourses.

Celia alternated between blaming herself and telling Roger it didn't matter. Each sexual encounter was a pass–fail test. When intercourse worked they were relieved, and when it didn't they were embarrassed and apologetic. Sex was no longer fun. Roger felt that sex wasn't worth it, and Celia said that was fine. However, Roger wanted sex in his life and felt guilty that when he masturbated he had easy erections. Why couldn't he get aroused with Celia? She particularly missed the touching and sensuality. They'd always been an affectionate couple, but other types of touching had been associated with a lead-up to intercourse. Celia was afraid that if intercourse was gone, all other touch would be gone too.

Roger and Celia went to the same internist, and it was Celia who asked for a Viagra prescription for Roger. The internist regularly prescribed Viagra but was medically conscientious enough to check to make sure that ED was not a symptom of a vascular or cardiac disease with Roger.

Roger hoped Viagra would return him to the predictable, easy erections of his 20s. Nothing from the ads he saw, written instructions about the drug, or what the doctor said disabused him of that unrealistic expectation. Celia was also naively optimistic. In fact, Viagra worked like it usually does, which is quite different than the miracle promised by the marketing hype. Roger was less controlled by anticipatory anxiety, and once he felt subjectively aroused his vascular system was more efficient and the erection was easier to maintain. His erectile and intercourse experiences returned to the pattern of 10 years previously, with a majority of encounters including intercourse. Celia was pleased, but not Roger. His sexual confidence did not improve. Why couldn't he return to total control and predictability? Was he the only man on the East Coast who was a Viagra failure?

After a disappointing experience, Roger locked himself in the bathroom and Celia heard him crying. Again, it was she who called the internist and obtained a referral for couple sex therapy. Celia was hopeful and Roger embarrassed as they went for their first appointment. Roger prided himself in being a careful consumer who researched all kinds of machines and services. However, he had not done that with ED or Viagra. When the therapist told them that the successful Viagra user had intercourse between 65–85% of encounters, Roger was truly shocked. He believed he was the only man who had failed to return to 100% easy, predictable erections promised by the advertising hype.

The therapist was respectful and empathic, and said that the real challenge for Roger and Celia was to adopt the Good Enough Sex model, which would allow them to be sexual in their 60s, 70s, and 80s. Roger needed to confront the drug company myth of perfect erections and perfect intercourse. He had to stay involved in the touching process, whether or not it flowed to intercourse. He could switch gears to an erotic non-intercourse scenario, a sensual scenario, or simply ask for a "raincheck." Roger had to confront the "intercourse-or-nothing" criterion and replace it with a variable, flexible approach of sharing pleasure. He needed to learn to be open to an erotic flow to intercourse rather than demanding intercourse be a pass–fail test of his sexuality.

Celia's role was not just to encourage Roger to take the medication, but to be his intimate, erotic friend. Rather than remain mired in naïve hopefulness, Celia could become an involved, aroused partner on whom Roger could "piggy-back" his arousal. She also needed to encourage Roger (or herself guide intromission) to transition to intercourse at high levels of subjective and objective arousal. Celia was receptive and responsive to switching to erotic, non-intercourse sex and cuddly, sensual scenarios if their eroticism did not flow to intercourse. In fact, Celia was particularly good at saying, "This is not going to be an intercourse night; let's just play sexually" without Roger feeling badly. Roger and Celia were able to integrate the pro-erection medications (Celia preferred Cialis because of the greater degree of freedom) into their couple style of intimacy, pleasuring, and eroticism.

What Works for You

When it comes to pro-sex medications, one size does not fit all. Some men and couples are great with Viagra; others do much better with Cialis. Other men prefer a penile injection, an external pump, or another pro-erection medication. We urge the couple to consult the urologist together to discuss what is best and how to successfully implement the chosen medical intervention. Some women and couples do well with a hormonal vaginal lubricant and others do much better with a water-based hypoallergenic, sensual lotion from their drugstore.

We advocate the psychobiosocial approach to sexuality in terms of integrating sexual medicines and external aides into your couple sexuality. Psychologically, each partner needs to be open and receptive to the medication/aide; utilize what you are comfortable with while dropping what you're not. Maintain positive, realistic expectations of what the medication/aide can do rather than expect it to do everything. Biologically and physiologically, choose a medication/aide that is most efficient and has the fewest side effects for you. Relationally, integrate the medication/aide into your couple sexual style, and do not treat it as a stand-alone intervention. Sex is an interpersonal process of sharing pleasure, eroticism, and intercourse. By its nature couple sexuality is variable and flexible. You are not a 100% guaranteed performance machine.

Let's be specific about the most common male resources—the pro-erection medications of Viagra, Levitra, and Cialis. The decision of which medication to use is as much based on the man and couple's comfort and preferences as the physiological mechanism of the medication. For example, couples who prefer a focused, predictable routine will probably do better with Viagra. Its sexual window of opportunity of 1–4 hours facilitates the sexual initiation process. The man and couple who enjoy playfulness and unpredictability are more likely to effectively utilize Cialis with its 30-minute to 36-hour window of opportunity.

The most common female aides are vaginal lubricants and a vibrator. Does the woman chose the lubricant, or is it a joint choice? Does she use the lubricant before starting the sexual encounter, or does she use the lubricant as part of the pleasuring process? Does the lubricant facilitate subjective arousal or is it to make intercourse comfortable (i.e., not painful)? If the woman decides to utilize a hormonal-based lubricant (or other medication as they become available), she can ask her mate to accompany her to the consultation with the gynecologist or endocrinologist to discuss the best medication and how to successfully implement it into their couple sexual style. Who controls vibrator stimulation—she or he? Is vibrator stimulation used to build arousal or to facilitate orgasm? Is vibrator stimulation used during intercourse or in non-intercourse sex?

Exercise: Integrating Medication or Aides Into Your Couple Sexual Style

Let's assume you have chosen to use a pro-sex medication or a sexual aide. Focus on how to successfully integrate this into your couple sexual style of intimacy, pleasuring, and eroticism so it enhances sexual function and satisfaction. Whether you decide on a pro-erection medication, testosterone gel or injection, a medication to lengthen ejaculatory control, or an estrogen/testosterone supplement to facilitate desire, you need to consult your internist, urologist, gynecologist, endocrinologist, or psychiatrist. You want to be sure the medication or aide is being used in a medically prudent manner, that there will not be unwanted side effects, or that a systemic medical problem is not being ignored.

Next, you need to clearly have for yourself and communicate to your partner a positive, realistic expectation for the medication. You should understand what you need to do to enhance the efficacy of the medication, and what type of sexual and emotional support you are asking from your partner. This is to counter the marketing ads that promote the medication as a stand-alone miracle cure. We suggest having this talk over the kitchen table or on a walk—not in bed while in the middle of lovemaking.

Planning and talking is the first step, but implementation is the focus of this exercise. Increasing comfort and developing psychosexual skills does not involve a one-shot, pass–fail test. It requires practice, constructive feedback, frequency, and refining for you to build comfort and confidence with integrating this new resource in couple intimacy, pleasuring, and eroticism.

Guidelines for successfully implementing a medication are even more important with the use of a sexual aide or external resource. Be clear about its positive, realistic role for your couple sexual style and equally clear about concerns of misuse—the partner feels left out of the process, sex becomes performance-oriented and mechanical, or the aide controls the person's sexual desire and response. The core guideline for implementation is to view the medication/aide as a positive resource that can be integrated into your sexual style.

Closing Thoughts

Our psychobiosocial model of couple sexuality encourages you to utilize all your psychological, physical, couple, and psychosexual skill resources to increase sexual function and satisfaction. For many individuals and couples a crucial resource is pro-sex medications and sexual aides. You can successfully integrate the medication/aide into your couple sexual style of intimacy, pleasuring, and eroticism so it enhances sexual function and satisfaction. Do not treat this as a stand-alone intervention or expect perfect sexual performance. Value variable, flexible sexuality and adopt the Good Enough Sex model of couple satisfaction.

CHAPTER **13**

Confronting Sex and Aging

You are a sexual person from the day you're born until the day you die. The good news is that you can enjoy couple sexuality in your 60s, 70s, and 80s. The bad news is that by age 65 one-third of couples have stopped being sexual, and by age 75 sex is over for more than two-thirds. The classic Masters and Johnson guideline of "use it or lose it" can motivate you to enjoy couple sexuality throughout your life.

As you age, the mantra of integrating intimacy, pleasuring, and eroticism comes to fruition. For sex to be comfortable and functional after 60, it needs to be more genuine. You need each other as intimate, erotic friends. This is a special challenge for men who learned that sex was autonomous. In truth, sexuality is an intimate, interactive process. You could be independent sexually in your 20s and 30s, but if sexuality is to be satisfying in your later years you need each other both emotionally and physically.

The other major challenge with aging is to adopt and enjoy the Good Enough Sex Model. Rather than emphasize predictability, control, and intercourse performance, you should learn to value variability, flexibility, and a pleasure-oriented approach to sexuality. As you age, intercourse remains an integral part of your couple sexual style, but it should not be regarded as the absolute goal of your sexuality. The new mantra is that the essence of sexuality is "desire, pleasure, and satisfaction." Older couples wisely realize that when the sexual encounter does not flow to intercourse, the partners can feel satisfied with an erotic, non-intercourse scenario or a cuddly, sensual scenario. Concepts involving bridges to desire, sexual options, integrating intimacy and eroticism, valuing pleasure over performance, and enjoying sex as a process of giving and receiving pleasure reach fruition with aging.

Rather than aging being about loss of sexuality, a healthy way to approach aging is accepting that you need each other as intimate and erotic partners, making your sexuality more genuine and human. Rather than mourn the loss of automatic erections, he can enjoy a sensual encounter, focus on pleasuring his partner, and be open and receptive to her touch to help him achieve arousal and erection. Rather than mourn the loss of the media image of beauty, she can accept her body image, enjoy sensual, playful, and erotic touch both for her arousal and his openness to her helping enhance his arousal. He can "piggy-back" his arousal on hers, with both valuing intimate, interactive sexuality.

Another challenge of aging is mind–body integration. You want to engage in good health habits because what is good for your physical body is good for your sexuality. As you age, your vascular and neurological systems remain functional, but they become less efficient. Hormonal changes are more dramatic for women than men. The interaction between hormonal changes and sexual response is complex and variable. Use and misuse of hormone replacement therapy and testosterone supplements is quite controversial. We suggest consulting an endocrinologist for a second opinion about your medical options to enhance desire and function by using hormones.

The good news is that aging itself has relatively little effect on sexual response. The bad news is that there is an increase in illness and use of medications as you age. In fact, the major biological cause of sexual dysfunction is side-effects of medication. The average 60-year-old is taking at least one medication. Illness and medication side-effects do not stop sexual function, but they do alter sexual response. Thus, if couple sex is to continue to be pleasurable and functional, psychological, relational, and psychosexual skill factors become more important to compensate for vulnerable physiology.

Psychologically, this means adopting a positive attitude toward the challenge of healthy sexuality with aging. Relationally, it means turning toward your partner as your intimate, erotic friend with whom to share pleasure, not perform for. The most important psychosexual factor is adopting the Good Enough Sex Model and accepting variable, flexible sexual response as the best kind of sex, especially with aging (although we advocate this as the best model for couple sexuality throughout their lives). It means focusing on relaxation, piggy-backing your arousal on your partner's, valuing sensual, playful, and erotic touch both for itself and as a bridge to sexual intercourse, transitioning to intercourse at high levels of arousal, using multiple stimulation during intercourse, accepting that 5–15% of encounters will be dissatisfying or dysfunctional, being a resilient sexual couple, valuing both mutual and one-way sex, and enjoying both intercourse and non-intercourse sexuality.

A favorite example of adapting to changes in your physical body is the couple who deals with one partner's chronic pain disorder. If a partner's body is most flexible and there is reduced pain between 9–11 a.m. or after a nap, that is the time to have a sexual encounter. Often, that is an entirely new sexual pattern. Partners need to go with their bodies and their comfort/receptivity pattern rather than fight against it. Another example is a couple with a long pattern of being sexual late at night. Now that they are retired at 72, the best time to be sexual may be in the morning when they are refreshed from a good night's sleep and testosterone levels and energy are at their highest. As you age, you can enjoy greater degrees of freedom and physical and sexual need for each other rather than mourn the loss of physical efficacy.

Gender Issues With Aging

The great majority of couples find that in their 20s and 30s male sexual response is easier, faster, and more reliable than female sexual response. Comedians gather much of their material from stereotypes about male–female differences in sexual desire and response. Across cultures and ages, the theme is that male sexuality is easy to elicit, while female sexuality is mysterious and complex. These gender and cultural differences not only change with aging, but sometimes there is a role reversal. The 60-year-old woman finds that her arousal is easier and more predictable than her 60-year-old male partner's. The wise male is open to "piggy-backing" his arousal on his female partner's rather than feeling competitive or panicky. Our theme is that as men and women age they need each other as intimate, erotic friends.

Tom and Alice   Tom and Alice are in a 42-year first marriage but, as Alice says, sexually there have been three marriages. The first sexual phase was the romantic love/passionate sex that started premaritally and extended into the first 18 months of the marriage. In retrospect, the quality of the sexual scenarios and techniques was not great, but the love and enthusiasm of finding a life partner drove the sex. The second phase was what Tom called "survival sex"—maintaining a sexual connection through the years of establishing family, career, and home. Alice has a less positive view. She recalls late-night sex squeezed into their busy lives as more a hassle than a pleasure. Tom and Alice do recall special sexual experiences, for example, their 20th wedding anniversary trip to Hawaii. However, the norm was functional, unremarkable sex.

Tom and Alice are now enjoying the third phase of their sexual marriage, which began in their mid-50s. Rather than experiencing the dreaded "empty nest" syndrome, they discovered that being a couple again was a breath of fresh air personally, relationally, and sexually. Alice especially found it liberating not to have children at home and be free of the worries that parents typically have about adolescent children. Sexually, the biggest change was that Tom needed her interest and stimulation for his arousal. Alice told him that she much preferred his "grown-up" erections to his "show-up" erections, which she viewed as being independent of her. Having sex as an intimate, interactive couple facilitated Alice's desire in a way that she had not felt in more 20 years. Her positive attitude and responsiveness made it much easier for Tom to accept changes in his sexual response. Rather than feeling threatened or competitive, Tom really enjoyed Alice's newfound sexual voice. He'd read that the major aphrodisiac was an involved, aroused partner. Tom found this to be true in this new phase of their couple sexual style.

Another major change was that Tom's sexual desire/arousal/orgasm had been very reliable and predictable. If he drank too much on occasion, this subverted sex, but otherwise he reliably ejaculated during intercourse. In one way Alice envied that, but also found it strange and frustrating. Even if Tom was fatigued, they were not feeling close, the scenario was dull, or there was a family crisis, "old predictable Tom" would be sexually functional. In the first phase of their sexual life, Alice was desirous/aroused/orgasmic about 80% of the time, but this had decreased to less than 50% in the second phase. Paradoxically, once the sexual encounter began, orgasm was relatively easy for Alice even though her desire and arousal were often low. Since she was orgasmic, Tom could not understand why Alice didn't value sex as much as he did.

During the current phase of sex and aging, Tom came to appreciate the variable, flexible approach to couple sexuality. Tom and Alice acknowledged that the best sexual encounters were when both of them felt desirous, aroused, and orgasmic. This was the most energizing sexual experience. However, they were aware and mature enough to accept that sometimes the sexual experience was better for one than the other, that sometimes the sex was okay but unremarkable, that at times the encounter did not culminate in intercourse but rather erotic, non-intercourse sex. Furthermore, there were times when theirs was a sensual rather than a sexual encounter. By far the most important lesson was to accept that 5–15% of sexual encounters were lousy. Alice had no problems with this, but Tom did. Alice's assurance that it was not a big deal and "don't sweat the small stuff" was helpful, but Tom was too much of a traditional male to easily accept dysfunctional sex.

Accepting their bodies with illnesses, medication side-effects, and physical vulnerabilities was a further challenge. Tom had to manage high blood pressure and gout, using both medication and adopting better health habits. Alice had to deal with fibromyalgia and joint pain, which sapped her energy. Rather than fighting against aging, they accepted their aging process, stayed physically active, and focused on good health habits. Alice and Tom wanted the aging phase of their sexual life to be something that energized them and added to couple intimacy. Alice had not felt that way about the second phase of their sexual life but realized she could not change the past, although she had learned from it. Alice and Tom were committed to maintaining a vital and satisfying sexuality into their 80s.

Illness, Medications, Side-Effects, and Aging

A pervasive myth among both professionals and the public is that aging itself decreases sexual desire and response. In truth, aging does not have a major negative impact. The real issue is that as your body ages, you are more vulnerable to acute and chronic illnesses. The medications to treat these illnesses have side-effects that impact sexual function. In approaching illness and sexuality, we suggest three guidelines. First, be an active, knowledgeable patient. This might include joining an illness self-help group or researching treatment/management options on the Internet.

Second, we encourage you to schedule a joint couple session with your internist or specialist to discuss couple sexual issues. There are several reasons why physicians avoid dealing with sexual problems: they have received minimal training in sexual medicine; sexual problems tend to be complex and medicine works best when there is an acute problem, a specific diagnosis, and a specific medical treatment; and they do not have the time or interest to do sexual counseling. However, if you go to a consultation as a couple and make it clear that you do not want sexual counseling but want to focus on the illness, medications, and health behaviors so you can reduce their impact on your sexuality, this will bring out the best in the physician. Third, be open to changing/reducing medications or changing health habits to reduce negative side effects and promote healthy sexuality. Remember the psychobiosocial Good Enough Sex Model. You want to promote a variable, flexible sexuality and reduce or eliminate factors that impede individual and couple sexual function.

Healthy sexuality is imbedded in a healthy body. You need not be in perfect physical health to enjoy healthy sexuality, but you do need to be an active person and adapt to your aging body. The chief guideline is to realize that illness and medication often do change sexual function, although they do not stop it. A crucial element in healthy aging is to enjoy intimacy and touching. Valuing intimacy, pleasuring, and eroticism is a prime resource in dealing with aging and attendant illness.

Exercise: Enjoying Sensual and Sexual Pleasure After 60

This exercise asks you to focus on the gains, challenges, and opportunities in sharing yourself and your body after 60. Emphasize what you can do to revitalize your couple sexual style so you can enjoy sex into your 80s. In this exercise, each of you initiates a pleasuring/eroticism encounter that incorporates new strategies and techniques to enhance sexual pleasure and satisfaction. A great advantage is that you have the time to enjoy a slowly building sensual and sexual response. You need each other more in terms of a genuine human connection. Being receptive and responsive to your partner's touch allows you to "piggy-back" your arousal on each other's. Does she enjoy helping him become aroused by seductive touch or direct penile stimulation? Can she accept that it is normal for him not to ejaculate each time? For many aging couples, female sexual response is easier and more predictable than his. How do each of you feel about this? Can you welcome and enjoy it?

How do you feel about emphasizing sensual and genital touch to encourage arousal rather than rely on visual stimulation and rapid response? Be open to changes in your body and sexual responsivity; share and accept these with your partner. Be open to using pleasuring techniques that include non-genital touching, a vaginal lubricant before or as part of the pleasuring process, manual and oral stimulation, different rhythms of touch and pleasuring, use of multiple stimulation before and during intercourse. What facilitates individual and mutual arousal? Enjoy a sexuality that is intimate and interactive, rather than automatic and performance oriented. You don't need to prove anything to yourself, your partner, or anyone else, but you do need to share yourself and pleasure each other. Celebrate your heightened sexual variability, sharing, and flexibility. Sexuality with aging is about enjoying an integrated, broad-based sexual experience. It may be less physically intense, but it can be more intimate, genuine, and fulfilling.

To complete the experience, bask in the afterplay phase. While holding and touching, discuss how pleasuring, erotic scenarios, intercourse, and afterplay can continue to be a vital part of your intimate relationship.

Closing Thoughts

Maintaining good physical health and health habits is important in maintaining sexuality in your 60s, 70s, and 80s. Even more important are psychological, relational, and psychosexual skill factors. The crucial psychological factor is a positive attitude of confronting and accepting challenges and valuing variable, flexible couple sexuality. The crucial relational factor is valuing each other as intimate and erotic friends. The key psychosexual skill factor is blending self-entrancement arousal and partner interaction arousal. In addition, some couples add role enactment arousal. The Good Enough Sex Model facilitates both pleasuring and erotic techniques flowing to intercourse at high levels of arousal. When sex doesn't flow to intercourse, the ability to accept and enjoy erotic, non-intercourse scenarios and sensual scenarios is crucial. The mantra of intimacy, pleasuring, and eroticism reaches its fruition with aging.

PART **IV**

Maintaining Healthy Couple Sexuality

CHAPTER 14

Nurturing Sexuality as Intimate, Erotic Friends

Hopefully, your mate is more than your sexual partner; he/she is your intimate friend. New relationships are all about anticipation, romance, passionate sex, idealization, and the drive to make this relationship fun, sexy, and successful. This is a special time for couples—the sex is spontaneous, romantic, and energetic. For most couples, this phase lasts between six months and two years.

Unfortunately, serious couples, whether married or not, become so preoccupied with managing day-to-day tasks involving jobs, parenting, household duties, community events, and life responsibilities that they treat their sexual relationship with benign neglect. They might be a functional sexual couple but lose the spark of emotional and sexual intimacy. Almost half of couples report that the best sex was during the first six months of the relationship, which is a loss for couple vitality and satisfaction.

You can make the transition from the romantic love/passionate sex/ idealization phase to develop an intimate, erotic couple sexual style so that sexuality remains a positive, integral part of your life and relationship. Sexual intimacy can energize your bond, and contribute 15–20% to relationship satisfaction. When partners see each other as both intimate and erotic friends, they have a special relationship resource, which helps maintain vitality and satisfaction. Good sex cannot compensate for a lack of respect, trust, or commitment—no matter what you hear on talk radio, see in movies, overhear in bars, or listen to in love songs. Healthy sexuality plays a positive, integral role in energizing your relationship and contributing 15–20% to relationship vitality and satisfaction. A comfortable, satisfying couple sexual style is an important contributor to relational vitality and security.

A crucial component of your intimate bond is fostering feelings of desire and desirability. The role for sexual intimacy is to energize your couple bond, to add a sense of specialness. Sexuality can serve a number of positive relational functions—a shared pleasure, a means to reinforce intimacy, a tension reducer, a way to strengthen self-esteem and feelings of attractiveness, and, of course, the traditional biological function of pregnancy with a planned, wanted child.

Sex can have a number of meanings. It's a way to affirm love; a port in the storm after a conflict with a child; a way to reconnect after a period of physical or emotional distance; a means to begin a family; a celebration after a move to a new house; a form of spiritual comfort after the death of a parent. Often sex plays a different role for one partner than the other. Not only is that normal, it is a positive function of couple sexuality. For one partner sex may be about the need for orgasm as a tension reducer; for the other sex means closeness and warmth. One partner might have sex for pregnancy, while the other emphasizes the pleasure of sex. Sex for one partner might involve a reaching out for affirmation; the other partner may find sex easy and nurturing. For some sex is a way to reinforce and deepen intimacy; for others it meets the need for playful touch. Couples who accept the multiple roles and meanings of sexuality have a variable, resilient couple sexual style that can be integrated into their daily lives.

Valuing Both Intimacy and Eroticism

Traditionally, intimacy was the woman's domain, and eroticism was the man's domain. Men were not supposed to be aware of, much less value, intimacy. The woman reacted to the man's eroticism; she wasn't supposed to have her own erotic voice. This is based on the assumption that men and women are totally different sexual species.

We have a substantially different concept of adult men and women, especially those involved in a serious or marital relationship. Psychologically, relationally, and sexually there are many more similarities than differences in healthy adult men and women. The most important concept is that both value intimacy and eroticism, and that the common goal of sex is relational satisfaction.

Men can and do value intimacy and touching, as do women. Women can and do value eroticism and orgasm, as do men. Rather than a war between the sexes, they have similar goals. Men and women are allies who join in the pursuit of sexual satisfaction.

Intimacy and eroticism are different, but complementary. Intimacy emphasizes closeness, safety, predictability, security, and a comfortable/safe connection. Eroticism emphasizes high levels of emotional and sexual arousal, taking personal and sexual risks, impulsivity and creativity, unpredictability, and a special, energizing connection. Ideally, both the man and woman value intimacy and eroticism, and integrate these into their couple sexual style. In fact, a core dimension of your couple sexual style is the particular balance of intimacy and eroticism that fits your individual and couple needs. The balance is uniquely yours, but both intimacy and eroticism are core components of healthy couple sexuality.

Sallie and Sean   Sean and Sallie's favorite wedding gift was a totally blank joke book, "The Irish Guide to Lovemaking." They were a well-educated Irish Catholic couple who were committed to not falling into the trap of that cultural stereotype. This was particularly important to Sean, who was pretty sure his parents were a non-sexual couple. Sean graduated from a Catholic college, and as an adult was a moderately religious, liberal Catholic who believed that Catholics had the most well-rounded, stable, and sexually-satisfying marriages. He wanted this in his marriage with Sallie. Sallie's father had died when she was eight, and although her mother was social and dated, she'd not remarried. Her mother liked Sean and wished Sallie the best, but was neither pro-marriage or pro-sex.

Like the majority of couples these days, Sallie and Sean cohabitated (for eight months) prior to marriage. They very much enjoyed the romantic love/passionate sex/idealization phase of their courtship and were not surprised that this was gone shortly after they began living together. In developing an intimate, erotic couple style, Sallie emphasized the intimacy and Sean the eroticism, but each realized the other's focus was important for a sexually healthy relationship.

For Sallie, the key to emotional and sexual intimacy was to feel safe with Sean and to develop a strong, resilient bond. For Sean, the key was feeling that Sallie was receptive and responsive to his touch and that she would value marital sex. They had attended a 10-session skill-based pre-marital program that was much better than what their parents or peers had. The notable exception was sexuality. Sex was treated in a light, joking manner that reinforced traditional gender stereotypes—a great disservice to couples.

On their own, they agreed to read the chapters on "Sexuality" and "Sexual Problems" from our book *Getting It Right the First Time*. Sallie found the exercise about non-demand touching and the role of touch in sexual desire particularly valuable. Sean found the exercise about preventing extra-marital affairs a tremendous resource. He believes that his father's pattern of high-opportunity/low-involvement affairs was the issue behind his parent's non-sexual marriage. Sean agreed to disclose to Sallie any high-risk situation or person, especially regarding work (he was in sales and did moderate travel). As long as this issue was open to discussion,

Sallie felt secure. She did not see herself at risk for a "comparison affair," but told Sean she would discuss any "slippery slope" with him.

The most empowering message from their pre-marital program was the importance of building a strong marital foundation and a mutually acceptable couple style during their first two years of marriage. They wanted a strong, resilient marital bond of respect, trust, and intimacy. The core skills taught in the program were dealing with differences, conflict resolution, and problem-solving. Sallie and Sean took a step further and talked about the importance of their couple sexual style, which would be congruent with their marital style.

How could they integrate Sallie's emphasis on intimacy and safety with Sean's emphasis on eroticism and sexual frequency? The key: avoiding a power struggle and affirming the relational value of both intimacy and eroticism. Sean initiated caring, non-demand touching. Sallie developed her sexual voice, which included erotic scenarios that involved R-rated videos and reading feminist erotica. They valued their complementary couple sexual style. Sallie's embrace of vital couple sexuality and Sean's embrace of non-demand pleasuring were important. They truly became both intimate and erotic friends.

Advantages and Potential Pitfalls of a Sexual Friendship

Whether married or unmarried, couples need to develop a view of each other as both intimate and erotic people. This integration of intimacy and eroticism replaces the romantic love/passionate sex charge of a couple's early relationship. If sexuality is to continue to play a 15–20% role in relationship vitality and satisfaction, it needs to include genuine desire/pleasure/satisfaction.

For many couples, especially non-married couples, this is easier said than done. It takes little for sex to degenerate into a power struggle rather than constitute a sharing, pleasurable, intimate team experience. When sex becomes, "If you really loved me, you would say yes to sex or you would do what I want sexually," your relationship is in trouble. "If you loved me, you would …" is a recipe for disaster. Relationships are based on a positive influence process, not demands and threats. Sex is neither a reward for good behavior nor a punishment for problematic behavior.

"Intimate coercion" has no place in your couple sexual style. Contingencies, threats, coercion, and intimidation poison intimacy. You cannot be intimate friends if you are afraid of your partner. This is why interpersonal violence or threats of retribution are so destructive for couple intimacy. It is normal to feel disappointed, frustrated, or upset with your partner occasionally, whether about sex or life issues. Touching is a core healthy way to heal from an argument or stop a downward couple pattern. Sexuality is a healthy way to rejoin or to say you are sorry. However, you cannot use arguments as "foreplay." This might occur occasionally, but if it becomes a pattern this will subvert both the relationship and sexuality.

The essence of being intimate, erotic friends is positive motivation, feeling safe and accepted, being receptive and responsive to pleasurable touch, remaining open to taking emotional and sexual risks, engaging in erotic playfulness, enjoying the intensity of the moment, going with the erotic flow, letting go physically and emotionally, and delight in the afterplay experience.

Exercise: Valuing Each Other as Intimate and Erotic Friends

Be personal and concrete about what intimacy and eroticism mean to each of you. Start with eroticism. Share with your partner your memory of her/him when you felt the most sexy, desirable, and turned on. Focus both on the actual erotic scenario and techniques, as well as what gave this experience special meaning and allowed you to let go and savor eroticism. What did you do to feel and invite eroticism? What did your partner feel and do to elicit your erotic expression? Did this experience focus primarily on self-entrancement arousal, partner interaction arousal, role enactment arousal, or some blending of all three arousal dimensions? Are there erotic scenarios and techniques that feel special to you? How important are your partner's feelings and eroticism in creating your own? Make one or two requests of your partner to enhance eroticism, which can become an integral part of your couple sexual style.

Now let's focus on intimacy. The core components of intimacy are feeling emotionally safe, close, warm, and physically and emotionally open. Intimacy involves acceptance, affectionate, and sensual touch—a way of being with each other in a warm, meaningful manner. Intimacy is about safety and closeness, not erotic scenarios and techniques. Each partner identifies the intimate experiences and feelings he or she most values. What types of touch facilitate intimate feelings—holding hands, hugging, kissing, lying together in a position of trust, giving or receiving a back or head rub, giving or receiving a sensual massage, enjoying a Jacuzzi together? What types of emotional feelings or expression allow greater intimate connection? For some, verbalizing facilitates intimacy, for others the key is silence or breathing in tandem. For some, the important emotion is feeling safe, for others it is predictability, and for still others it is feelings of acceptance. What facilitates intimacy for you personally and as a couple? Share this awareness and understanding of the different roles and meanings of intimacy and eroticism. Now is the time to integrate them into your couple bond, enjoying both the closeness and the sexual energy.

Accepting Differences

Ideally, each partner experiences the same intimate and erotic feelings at each encounter. This is the stuff of love songs and movies. But it is not the reality for most couples most of the time. It is normal and healthy to have different experiences of intimacy and eroticism over time, including during a specific sexual encounter. Enjoy the variability and flexibility of healthy couple sexuality. All couples experience variability in their intimate and erotic feelings and encounters. Revel in this rather than worry or argue about it. Sex is not about being a mechanical performance machine or a comparison with a romantic love movie. Sex is about developing your unique couple sexual style that incorporates both intimacy and eroticism in your special way.

Closing Thoughts

Both intimacy and eroticism are essential to your couple sexual style. These are complementary, not adversarial, ways to express a vital, satisfying couple relationship. The trap to avoid is the traditional male–female power struggle in which men value eroticism and women value intimacy, which results in attacking your partner with "You don't get it." In truth, intimacy does interfere with "hook-up" sex, and eroticism will not nurture a sense of safety and connection in an emotionally alienated relationship. Married couples or those in a serious relationship can value intimacy and eroticism. The male can be an intimate partner, and the female can value erotic scenarios and techniques. This integration is the heart of deeply satisfying, interactive couple sexuality. The challenge for couple sexual satisfaction is to value your unique integration of intimacy and eroticism.

CHAPTER **15**
Maintaining Sexual Vitality

Having a sexual encounter that rivals a Hollywood movie is a fantastic experience, but for real-life couples maintaining a satisfying sexual relationship is the real payoff. Sex that energizes your couple bond, plays a 15–20% role in maintaining relationship vitality and satisfaction, and is a special experience of sharing pleasure and facilitating desire and desirability is key to healthy couple sexuality. Maintaining a comfortable, pleasurable, and satisfying couple sexual style allows you to integrate intimacy, pleasuring, and eroticism so that couple sexuality remains both strong and resilient.

Just as important is a sexual style that promotes vitality throughout your relationship, including into your 60s, 70s, and 80s. When Barry teaches his undergraduate Human Sexual Behavior class to 20- and 21-year-olds, only one in four can imagine their parents still having sex, and only one in thirteen believes that people of their grandparent's age are sexually active. That negative image of adult sexuality is disheartening, even though it's untrue. The good news is that if you maintain your couple sexual style you can take pride in beating the odds and enjoying intimacy, pleasure, and eroticism into your 80s.

Once established, few couples change their preferred sexual style. However, they do refine couple sexuality and accept and adapt to life changes, including being a couple with no children at home and coping with illness, retirement, and the aging process. It is in your best interest individually and as a couple to maintain a vital sexuality throughout your life.

The question inherent in this chapter is how to prevent your couple sexual style from becoming routine and mediocre. How can you maintain vital couple sexuality today and in the future? The authors have been married for more than 40 years and still do not take our intimate, erotic relationship for granted. For sexuality to play a vibrant role in relationship satisfaction you need to continue to invest time, psychological energy, and be open to new intimate and erotic scenarios. As we've said throughout the book, the real challenge for couples, married or unmarried, is to integrate intimacy and eroticism and to value a vital couple sexuality.

The traditional couple advice was to focus on intimacy, feeling close, and loving. Browsing through a book store reveals that the major emphasis is on eroticism. Books and articles tout the purported keys to sexual happiness: have mind-blowing sex 365 days a year, guarantee multi-orgasmic response every time, or do five things to ensure that your partner experiences the ultimate ecstasy. The message today is based on the crucial importance of perfect sexual performance—how to make your own porn movie. This sells a lot of books and magazines but does nothing to help real-life couples. In fact, if you take this advice seriously it can actually damage your sexual acceptance and satisfaction.

The truth is that healthy couple sexuality is based on comfort and acceptance, not proving something to yourself, your partner, or anyone else. Sexuality is about giving and receiving pleasure, not giving an R-rated, X-rated, or any other type of erotic performance. Your couple sexual style is based on variability, flexibility, and uniqueness. Contrary to the sexual hype, not everything works for everyone. The promise of ultimate satisfaction every time is intimidating, not empowering. The key is maintaining positive, realistic expectations, not buying into the "erotic hype."

It is essential to maintain balance between intimacy and eroticism— between being safe/close and sexually charged/adventurous, between being caring/generous and sexually focused, between emphasizing mutuality and self-focus. Relationships based solely on intimacy, as well as those based solely on eroticism, eventually stall out. If your goal is to maintain a vital, resilient couple sexuality, you need to value a balance of intimacy and eroticism.

Maintaining a healthy couple sexual style is more important than building your couple sexual style. A special value of an intimate relationship is its sense of acceptance and security. The role of sexuality is to energize your bond, enhance feelings of desire and desirability, and play a 15–20% role in relationship satisfaction. The paradox of sexuality is that sexual dysfunction, conflict, and avoidance can subvert or even threaten your relationship, but that good sex cannot substitute or compensate for a lack of respect, trust, or commitment.

Maintaining Sexual Gains and Preventing a Relapse

It is virtually useless to resolve sexual dysfunction and develop a couple sexual style unless you have a plan to maintain a healthy couple sexuality and to prevent relapse. These are our ten recommended relapse prevention strategies and techniques. We urge you to discuss them with your partner and commit to implementing the two to four that are particularly relevant for you. Maintaining gains and preventing relapse involves an active process of implanting strategies and techniques, not a passive process of hoping for the best.

1. Have couple meetings.

   Establish regular times (for example, on a 45-minute walk or over lunch once a month) to discuss the state of your intimate relationship. This facilitates maintaining couple identity and satisfaction. The message is that you want to regularly commit the time and psychological energy to nurture and enhance your couple sexual style.

2. Schedule a formal six-month couple meeting.

   Remain committed to maintaining a satisfying couple sexual style and preventing relapse by ensuring that you do not slip back into unhealthy sexual attitudes, behaviors, or feelings. You cannot treat couple sexuality with benign neglect. We suggest you set a new sexual goal for the next six months: Experiment with a new pleasuring sequence or intercourse position; go away as a couple without the children for a weekend; try three body lotions to determine which is most sensual; play out an erotic scenario like meeting at a convention and finding a place to be sexual; go to a church weekend program for couples to enhance spiritual and sexual meaning. At the next six-month couple meeting, talk about how this is progressing and set a new goal for the next six months.

3. Enjoy pleasuring sessions.

   Whether once every six weeks or once every four months, we suggest setting aside time for a pleasuring session (with a prohibition on intercourse and orgasm). This reinforces a comfortable, sensual, playful, flexible approach to giving and receiving pleasure-oriented touch without sexual performance demands. Allow yourself to experiment with and enjoy sensuality. You can do mutual touching or take turns, talk or be silent, read romantic poetry or sexy scenes from a novel. Anticipation is the key to desire, and sensuality is the key to sexual response.

4. Accept lapses as normal; don't allow a lapse to become a relapse.

   In movies and love songs, there is never a sexual problem. In real life, 5–15% of couple experiences are dissatisfying or dysfunctional. The real test of a positive, resilient couple sexuality is your ability to accept a dissatisfying/dysfunctional encounter and deal with it as an intimate team without guilt or blaming. Have a sexual experience in the following one to three days when you are receptive and responsive, not to compensate for the negative experience but to enjoy the pleasures of sexuality. When there is a negative sexual experience, it is normal to have automatic, self-doubting thoughts such as, "We're back at square one; I'm a sexual failure; what is wrong with us?" While occasional negative thoughts are to be expected, individually and as a couple you need to confront them and reaffirm that these fears are no longer valid. You can feel comfortable and confident in your couple sexual style. Your progress is real, not a lucky fluke. Your success becomes believable to both of you. You have learned the attitudes and psychosexual skills of cooperation and intimacy.

When you are tested by a dissatisfying/dysfunctional experience, what is important is that you address the challenge together. Accept the lapse and don't allow it to become a relapse. Utilize all your cognitive, behavioral, emotional, and relational skills to cooperate as an intimate team to focus on sexuality as a shared pleasure.

5. Establish positive, realistic sexual expectations.

Hopefully, by now you've discarded the criterion of movie-quality romantic love/passionate sex. If sexuality is to remain healthy and foster your intimate bond, your expectations need to remain both positive and realistic. Reasonable expectations allow you to integrate sex into real life, with its built-in fluctuations of sexual quality as you encounter stresses in your job, cope with the hands-on realities of parenting, deal with colds and fatigue, or experience lack of privacy in your house when there are visitors or extended family. Positive, realistic expectations include adopting a broad-based, flexible approach to touching and eroticism. You as a couple need to work cooperatively to find ways to accommodate each other's needs, wants, and preferences in a respectful, caring manner. Sexuality can meet a variety of individual and couple needs, including sex as a tension reducer, a way to share closeness and experience passion and orgasm, a way to heal after an argument, a bridge to reduce emotional distance, a means to be playful or to facilitate sleep. Most sex is mutual, but it is often better for one partner than the other. Vital sexuality is genuine, variable, and flexible.

6. Schedule intimate couple time.

The importance of setting aside quality couple time cannot be emphasized enough. You need a commitment to nurture couple intimacy. This is of special importance for couples with children. The husband–wife bond is the core of your family. You are better people and parents when you value each other as intimate partners. Many couples fall into the trap of not going away without the children for years at a time. We encourage you to schedule a couple weekend (or even an overnight) without children. At least once a year go away just as a couple, not with relatives or couple friends. In your daily life regular couple time can include going for a walk, having a sexual date, going out to dinner, sitting on the deck, or taking a half-hour nap and then enjoying a sensual or erotic encounter. Remember, your couple bond is the most important in the family.

7. Let your couple sexual style develop over time.

   You can develop your unique style of initiation, pleasuring, eroticism, intercourse, and afterplay. Once this style is established, don't treat couple sexuality with benign neglect. Remain open to adding to and refining your couple sexuality. Try a different pleasuring sequence or a sensual lotion, play out a role enactment scenario, try a different intercourse position or type of thrusting, or be more involved and caring during afterplay. The more flexible your couple sexual style and the more you accept the multiple functions of touching and sexuality, the greater your resistance to relapse. Develop a comfortable, functional, satisfying sexual style that meets both of your needs, and is flexible enough to adapt to changes in your lives. Your couple sexuality can continue to energize your relationship.

8. Be aware that Good Enough Sex varies in quality.

   The core of positive, realistic sexual expectations is the acceptance that if half of your sexual encounters are very satisfying for both of you, you have beaten the odds and have better sex than the majority of couples. Equally important is the acceptance that it is normal for 5–15% of encounters to be dissatisfying or dysfunctional. In fact, the single most important technique in relapse prevention is to accept and not overreact to disappointing or dysfunctional sexual experiences. Couples can accept that it is normal on occasion to experience inhibited desire, lose an erection, feel too fatigued for sex, experience premature ejaculation, do not have an orgasmic response, have sexual pain, or miscommunicate about a sexual date. Couples who accept sexual variability without panicking or blaming will have a strong, resilient couple sexual style. Dissatisfying/dysfunctional encounters occur among the most loving couples. Take pride in having a resilient couple sexual style.

9. Saturate each other with pleasurable touch.

   Sexual intimacy is much more than intercourse. You need a variety of intimate and erotic ways to connect, reconnect, and maintain couple intimacy. Be aware of the value for you and your relationship of affectionate, sensual, playful, erotic, and intercourse touch. The more ways you have to maintain an intimate and sexual connection, the easier it is to avoid relapse and enjoy vital, resilient couple sexuality.

10. Expand your sexual repertoire.

A flexible sensual and erotic repertoire is a major antidote to relapse. Touching and sexuality that meets a range of feelings, needs, and situations will serve your couple sexual style well and support your emotional and sexual gains. Couples with a flexible repertoire express intimacy through massage, holding hands, showering together, enjoying playful touch, cuddling on the couch while watching a DVD, and enjoying semi-clothed or nude sensual touch. You can maintain a vital sexual relationship by being open to planned as well as spontaneous sexual encounters, prolonged and varied erotic scenarios, or "quickies." You can experiment with intercourse positions, try self-entrancement or role enactment arousal, and use multiple stimulation during intercourse. Be open to adding something new to your sexual repertoire every six months. For example, try a new sensual lotion, a different sequence for a sensual or erotic scenario, a new intercourse position, multiple stimulation, or a new afterplay scenario.

Closing Thoughts

In movies and novels, once sex problems are resolved, the couple lives happily ever after. In reality, you cannot take your couple sexual style for granted; nor can you rest on your laurels. We advocate an active relapse prevention program and, if sexuality gets off track, a problem-solving approach. Why waste psychological energy dealing with a crisis when you can more efficiently and happily prevent the reappearance of sexual problems?

The more broadly based and resilient your couple sexual style—with an emphasis on sharing intimacy, pleasure, and eroticism—the more likely you will continue to enjoy satisfying sexuality. Choose the relapse prevention strategies and techniques that are most relevant to you and make them an ongoing part of your sexual life. You want to enjoy couple sexuality throughout your life.

As strongly as we can, we encourage you to maintain and generalize your intimacy and erotic gains. You deserve to have sexuality energize your intimate relationship so that it continues to play a special role in your life. Take pride and enjoyment in creating and maintaining your sexual style.

APPENDIX **A**

Choosing an Individual, Couple,
or Sex Therapist

This is a self-help book, but it is not a do-it-yourself therapy book. Individuals and couples are often reluctant to consult a therapist, feeling that to do so is a sign of craziness, a confession of inadequacy, or an admission that your life and relationship are in dire straits. In reality, seeking professional help is a sign of psychological wisdom and strength. Entering individual, couple, or sex therapy means that you realize there is a problem, and you have made a commitment to resolve the issues and promote individual and couple growth.

The mental health field can be confusing. Couples therapy and sex therapy are clinical subspecialties. They are offered by several groups of professionals, including psychologists, marital therapists, psychiatrists, social workers, and pastoral counselors. The professional background of the practitioner is less important than his or her competence in dealing with your relational and sexual health and addressing specific problems.

Many people have health insurance that provides coverage for mental health and thus can afford the services of a private practitioner. Those who do not have either the financial resources or insurance could consider a city or county mental health clinic, a university or medical school outpatient mental health clinic, or a family services center. Some clinics have a sliding fee scale based on your ability to pay.

When choosing a therapist, be assertive in asking about credentials and areas of expertise. Ask the clinician what the focus of the therapy will be, how long therapy can be expected to last, and whether the emphasis is specifically on sexual problems or more generally on individual, communications, or relationship issues. Be especially diligent in asking about credentials such as university degrees and licensing. Be wary of people who call themselves personal counselors, sex counselors, or personal coaches. There are poorly qualified persons—and some outright quacks—in any field.

One of the best ways to obtain a referral is to call a local professional organization such as a state psychological association, marriage and family therapy association, or mental health association. You can ask for a referral from a family physician, clergyman or rabbi, or trusted friend. If you live near a university or medical school, call to find out what mental and sexual health services may be available.

For a sex therapy referral, contact the American Association of Sex Educators, Counselors, and Therapists (AASECT) through the Internet at http://www.aasect.org or write or call for a list of certified sex therapists in your area: P.O. Box 1960, Ashland, VA 23005; phone: (804) 752-0026. Another resource is the Society for Sex Therapy and Research (SSTAR) at http://www.sstarnet.org.

For a marital therapist, check the Internet site for the American Association for Marriage and Family Therapy (AAMFT) at http://www .therapistlocator.net or the Association for Behavioral and Cognitive Therapies (ABCT) at http://www.abct.org. Another good resource is the national Registry of Marriage Friendly Therapists, who are dedicated to helping marriages succeed if possible: http://www.marriagefriendlythera pists.com. If you are looking for a psychologist who can provide individual therapy for anxiety, depression, behavioral health, or other psychological issues, we suggest the National Registry of Health Service Providers in Psychology: http://www.findapsychologist.org.

Feel free to talk with two or three therapists before deciding with whom to work. Be aware of your level of comfort with the therapist, degree of rapport, whether the therapist has special skill working with couples, and whether the therapist's assessment of the problem and approach to treatment makes sense to you. Once you begin, give therapy a chance to be helpful. There are few miracle cures. Change requires commitment, and it's a gradual and often difficult process. It takes time to change attitudes, feelings, and behavior. Although some people benefit from short-term therapy (fewer than 10 sessions), most find the therapeutic process will require four months or longer. The role of the therapist is that of a consultant rather than a decision maker. Therapy requires effort, both during the session and at home. It takes courage to seek professional help, but therapy can be of tremendous value in evaluating and changing individual, relational, and sexual problems.

Sexual Health Books and Resources

Suggested Reading on Couple Sexuality

Holstein, L. (2002). *How to have magnificent sex: The seven dimensions of a vital sexual connection.* New York: Harmony Books.

McCarthy, B., & McCarthy, E. (2003). *Rekindling desire.* New York: Brunner/Rutledge.

Perel, E. (2006). *Mating in captivity.* New York: HarperCollins.

Suggested Reading on Male Sexuality

McCarthy, B., & Metz, M. (2008). *Men's sexual health.* New York: Routledge.

Metz, M., & McCarthy, B. (2003). *Coping with premature ejaculation: Overcome PE, please your partner, and have great sex.* Oakland, CA: New Harbinger.

Metz, M., & McCarthy, B. (2004). *Coping with erectile dysfunction: How to regain confidence and enjoy great sex.* Oakland, CA: New Harbinger Publications.

Milsten, R., & Slowinski, J. (1999). *The sexual male: Problems and solutions.* New York: W. W. Norton.

Zilbergeld, B. (1999). *The new male sexuality.* New York: Bantam Books.

Suggested Reading on Female Sexuality

Foley, S., Kope, S., & Sugrue, D. (2002). *Sex matters for women: A complete guide to taking care of your sexual self.* New York: Guilford.

Heiman, J., & LoPiccolo, J. (1988). *Becoming orgasmic: Women's guide to sexual fulfillment.* New York: Prentice-Hall.

Other Notable Sexuality Readings

Fisher, H. (2004). *Why we love*. New York: Henry Holt.

Glass, S. (2003). *Not "just friends."* New York: Free Press.

Joannides, P. (2006). *The guide to getting it on*. West Hollywood, CA: Goofy Foot Press.

Maltz, W. (2001). *The sexual healing journey*. New York: HarperCollins.

Maltz, W. (2006). *Passionate hearts: The poetry of sexual love* (2nd ed.). New York: New World Library.

Michael, R., Gagnon, J., Laumann, E., & Kolata, G. (1994). *Sex in America: A definitive survey*. New York: Little, Brown.

Snyder, D., Baucom, D., & Gordon, K. (2007). *Getting past the affair*. New York: Guilford.

Vaughn, P. (2008). *Preventing affairs*. San Diego: Dialog Press.

Suggested Reading on Relationship Satisfaction

Chapman, G. (1995). *The five love languages: How to express heartfelt commitment to your mate*. Chicago: Northfield Publishing.

Doherty, W. (2001). *Take back your marriage*. New York: Guilford.

Gottman, J. (1999). *The seven principles for making marriage work*. New York: Crown Publishing.

Harrar, S., & DeMaria, R. (2006). *The seven stages of marriage*. New York: Reader's Digest Books.

Johnson, S. (2008). *Hold me tight*. Boston: Little Brown.

Love, P., & Stosny, S. (2006). *How to improve your marriage without talking about it*. New York: Broadway Books.

Markman, H., Stanley, S., & Blumberg, S. (2001). *Fighting for your marriage: Positive steps for preventing divorce and preserving a lasting love*. San Francisco: Jossey-Bass.

McCarthy, B., & McCarthy, E. (2004). *Getting it right the first time: Creating a healthy marriage*. New York: Brunner/Routledge.

McCarthy, B. W., & McCarthy, E. (2006). *Getting it right this time*. New York: Routledge.

Professional Associations

American Association for Marriage and Family Therapy (AAMFT): http://www.therapistlocator.net

American Association of Sex Educators, Counselors, and Therapists (AASECT): P.O. Box 1960, Ashland, VA 23005. Phone (804) 752-0026, http://www.aasect.org

Association for Behavioral & Cognitive Therapies (ABCT): 305 Seventh Avenue, New York, NY 10001-6008. Phone (212) 647-1890, http://www.abct.org

Sex Information and Education Council of the United States (SIECUS): 130 West 42nd Street, Suite 350, New York, NY 10036. Phone (212) 819-7990, fax (212) 819-9776, http://www.seicus.org

Smart Marriages: http://www.smartmarraige.com

Society for Sex Therapy and Research (SSTAR): http://www.sstarnet.org

Videotapes and Sexual Enrichment

Good Vibrations Mail Order: 938 Howard Street, Suite 101, San Francisco, CA 94110. Phone (800) 289-8423, http://www.goodvibes.com

Sex: A lifelong pleasure series (1991). Available from the Sinclair Institute, P.O. Box 8865, Chapel Hill, NC 27515. Phone 1 (800) 955-0888.

Sommers, F. *The great sex video series.* (Available from Pathway Productions, Inc., 360 Bloor Street West, Suite 407A, Toronto, Canada M5S 1X1).

Stubbs, K. R. (1994). *Erotic massage.* (Available from the Secret Garden, P.O. Box 67, Larkspur, CA 94977).

The couples guide to great sex over 40, vols. 1 and 2 (1995). Available from the Sinclair Institute, P.O. Box 8865, Chapel Hill, NC 27515. Phone 1 (800) 955-0888.